Advance Praise for *What's On Your Sign?*

"If you want to make a positive difference in the world but aren't sure where to start, then read this book. Don't just read it, but also go through the exercises that Terri Lyon has carefully prepared. If you put in the time and effort, these exercises will lead you to your purpose in life and show you how to be an effective advocate for the cause that is dearest to your heart."
~ Wendy Werneth, author of *Veggie Planet* and creator of The Nomadic Vegan

"I have spent my life passion on making a difference in the world with peace always at the forefront of my heart. Terri Lyon has written a thoughtful and intentional book that will serve as a valuable gift to all who take time to read and internalize her message of 'claiming' what you choose to write on your sign. In gratitude."
~Kathleen Puckett, Mental Health Professional, and Political Activist

"If you are looking for an easy to read, beginner's guide to becoming an activist, Terri Lyon has written "What's on Your Sign" just in time. Terri shares her own journey of wanting to ultimately create a positive impact in the world. She describes the process for herself, a self-identified "unexpected activist" (and other types of activists), in great detail. The reader will discover valuable tools designed to support the strategic examination of personal gifts, values, motivations, and opportunities as they set and achieve activism goals. In the current climate, many of us are searching for purposeful action that positively impacts the causes about which we care. This guidebook for activists will illuminate your path!"
~Dr. Rebecca Lucas, LGBTQ Activist, Advocate, Trainer, and Professor

"I learned so much from Terri Lyon's book What's on Your Sign: How to focus your passion and change the world. I am not a sign-toting, march-going activist but through her book I found ways to bring change in the places that matter to me in a way that works for my personality. I felt inspired and encouraged due to her step-by-step layout from finding my passion to making a difference. This is more than a go-get-em type of book. It has practical steps and ideas that bring you through the process if you are a beginner activist or someone who needs an infusion of centered focus. Terri has brought her years of teaching into the world of social justice. I am excited to hear about the things you will accomplish when you put her steps into practice."
~Dr. Catherine Denton, author of *Metaphysical Girl: How I Recovered My Mental Health*

What's On Your Sign?

How to focus your passion and change the world

Terri L. Lyon

What's On Your Sign? How to focus your passion and change the world
Written by Terri L. Lyon

Cataloging Information
Lyon, Terri
What's On Your Sign? How to focus your passion and change the world
/Terri L. Lyon
ISBN: 978-0-9980-3240-5
Self-Help-Personal Growth-General
Social Science-Volunteer Work

For information contact: admin@lifeattheintersection.com
https://www.WhatsOnYourSign.com
Book and Cover design by JP Luna
Editing by Trish Richert
Author Photos by © Mark Empey Photography
First Edition: November 2018
Printed in the United States of America
10 9 8 7 6 5 4 3 2 1

Dedication

I dedicate this book to those who came before me.

Contents

Introduction

Each moment from all sides rushes to us the call to love.
We are running to contemplate its vast green field.
Do you want to come with us?
This is not the time to stay at home,
but to go out and give yourself to the rose garden.
The dawn of joy has arisen,
and this is the moment of vision. ~Rumi

I'M THE ONLY LIBERAL in a band of right-leaning geniuses. The youngest of five children, for a long time I yearned to be like my accomplished parents and older siblings.

My father, a brilliant WWII Marine, joined U.S. Steel as a shipping clerk and retired as a plant manager. Since my father worked long hours, my mother managed our home. As a toddler, I would lie awake and fret that she might die, so I would pad down the stairs and sit with her. Playing with her bony fingers while she read, I'm sure she saw me as a nuisance during her rare time alone. A fierce champion of her kids, when my friends picked me for the role of Maid in our Princesses game, she sent me in my sister's sparkly prom dress. Knee-length for my sister, floor length for me, with tulle underneath; my friends promoted me to Queen.

My sister was a cheerleader, prom queen, fantastic mother, and the force behind a city-provided after-school care program. My brothers are high-achievers, too, academically and in their business lives.

But families are complicated. My parents weren't loud and ugly bigots. But there were many mixed messages. My mother taught me to love my siblings even when I didn't like them. But, because of WWII, she also wanted me to hate Japanese people. Her refusal to buy a Japanese-made TV led to a hilarious but unsuccessful quest for an American model.

My father was a predictable man; you could set your watch for 5 p.m. when he opened the bourbon bottle. I would run to cuddle under his arm as he watched TV and drank for the rest of the evening. He was always nicer at night. He taught me to follow through on my commitments, and how to play golf and ping-pong. But he also told me I must go to college in case my husband left me. I'd need a job.

I have no idea how I ended up a liberal despite the influence of my family. Maybe because they shrugged off my questions, such as why I couldn't play with the Polish kids who moved in down the street. Or because they ridiculed me if I spoke up with ideas that didn't fit into their worldview. By kindergarten I was afraid to share my views; in my report card my teacher wrote, "Please ask Terri to speak up." I didn't speak up for decades.

I hunkered down and pretended the things they said and did were normal. My mother cried for days because I was zoned to a school in the "bad part of town." My parents refused to shelter my father's secretary's young boys when she begged to get them out of Nicaragua during the dangerous Sandinista revolt. After my engagement to my boyfriend Pat, whose father is Hispanic, a family member called me, not to offer congratulations but to say, "So I hear you are marrying a spic."

People who are supposed to love me say with contempt, "You're such a liberal." It is confusing when you don't share the same beliefs as your family. I know it is possible to love someone just as they are and honor your differences. But in my family, anything liberal disgusted them, so I wondered if I disgusted them too. I still wonder.

I shielded my husband and kids from the worst of my extended family. Our staunch rule at family reunions to avoid religion or politics usually resulted in quasi-decent behavior. But my husband caught on, of course, and one day asked, "How did you come out of that family?" I don't know the answer. Either I was born that way, or my circumstances formed me. But whatever the reason, I'm ashamed and embarrassed I stayed quiet for so long.

Wake-Up Call

On November 7, 2016, I got a wake-up call.

I didn't watch on election night, thinking that the next day the nightmare would be over, and life would be normal again. But I woke up at 3 a.m. and decided to check the results. *The Washington Post* website showed a Trump win; I thought it was a joke. I checked several other sites, but nothing changed. My heart began to ache.

Seared into my brain is the cartoon Trump on the election results site. It anchors my life story now in the same way as hearing about Reagan's shooting on the car radio. Like learning about the Space Shuttle Challenger explosion while sitting among students in a middle school cafeteria. Like watching the second plane hit the World Trade Center. These anchors remind me that my world changed at that moment.

Becoming an Unexpected Activist

After my wake-up call, I became an unexpected activist. I'd been hiding and letting others do the arduous work of making change. But on election night I decided I wasn't going to be afraid to speak up anymore.

Surprisingly, I wasn't. My son and I went to the 2017 Women's March on Washington. Although we knew it might be dangerous, my son summed it up, "If we get hurt it will probably be worth it." I wrote the Legal Aid number on my arm in Sharpie, but I wasn't sure what to put on my protest sign; crafting a heartfelt, focused message seemed impossible because there were countless issues to fight. I didn't take a protest sign, but the ones I saw enchanted me. The protestors inspired me to get clear about my fight.

When I got back from DC, I finally decided what to do.

Research. Most activists head to the streets, but I went to the library. Since I felt such love for books, I was sure they would tell me the two things I wanted to know about activism—how to get started and how to be effective. They didn't. Most books are for those who are sure of their issue. And there is little research on what activism methods work.

When I didn't find what I was looking for—easy-to-use, evidence-based methods for getting started in activism—I decided to write *What's On Your Sign?* to document what I learned from my research; I also drew on my background in Industrial and Organizational Psychology and my experience in government, manufacturing, and teaching. I outlined a process for new activists and used the method to find my way into activism. *What's On Your Sign?* is for people like me, who are ready to make change and need a research-based guide to channeling their passion into the change they want to make in the world.

Use the tools in this book to focus your passion, pinpoint the gifts you bring to activism, and find the right activism opportunity. As the Sufi mystic poet Rumi says, "Now is not the time to stay home." Open the door, step out, and start the challenging work of making change. With *What's On Your Sign?* you have a map to explore your activism path.

You will:

- ~ Find your passion.
- ~ Identify the skills you have for making change.
- ~ Inventory your knowledge.
- ~ Understand your motivation and how it affects your activism.
- ~ Find activism that works.
- ~ Craft your ideal activism opportunity.
- ~ Make an impact, get energized, use your gifts, and grow as an activist.
- ~ Set goals to stay motivated and check your impact.

Because of the many issues to fight, you must narrow your focus. Once you do, you'll find the right match of your gifts to the change you want to see. I hope my book will help you get clear about the change you want to make in the world and how to start.

Your Protest Sign

When I started my activism journey, I wanted to carry a protest sign, but I had no idea what message to display. But with the process outlined in this book, I know the change I want to make, and I can do it.

What's On Your Sign? Before you step into the crowd, what heartfelt message for change do you scrawl on your protest sign?

This book will help you find out.

PART 1

Your Passion

In Part 1 of *What's On Your Sign?* focus on your passion. Create a vision for your life. Imagine the world as you wish to see it. Choose the change you want to make to move closer to your ideal world. Doing this work up front means a better match with the activism opportunities you will explore later.

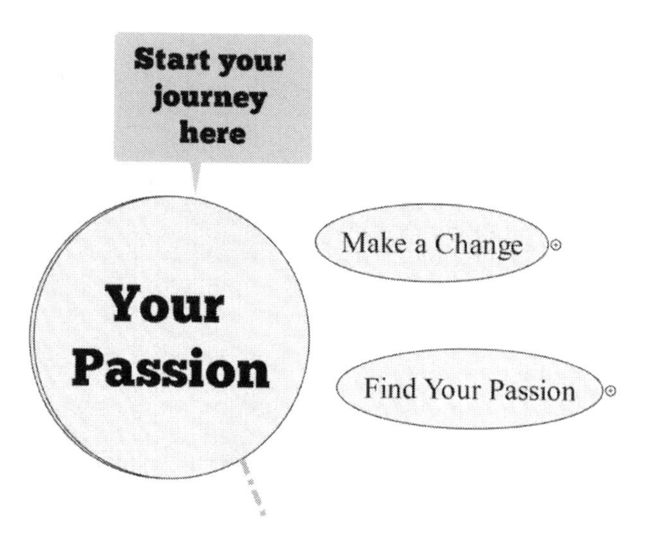

Part 1 includes:

Chapter 1: Make a Change

Chapter 2: Find Your Passion

CHAPTER 1

Make a Change

You'll never do a whole lot unless you're brave enough to try. ~Dolly Parton [1]

Objective

Identify the type of activist you most resemble.

Goal

Identify the type of activist you most resemble and which sections of *What's On Your Sign?* will help you.

YOU DOUBTLESS HAVE A COPY of your resumé hanging around just in case you want to change jobs. Your resumé is a documented, organized, and concise summary of what you bring to a new position.

Use a similar approach for activism. Be explicit about your skills, knowledge, and motivation you can use to make a difference and find the right activism opportunity. When you understand your gifts, you can share them with others.

What Do I Mean by Activism?

Before I go further, I'd like to distinguish activism from related terms. Activism is "the act of influencing a person or group with the goal of eliciting a desired behavioral change."[2] This definition goes beyond educating someone about an issue toward encouraging a difference in behavior.

Other terms are used interchangeably with activism. *Advocacy* is the act of influencing a person or group toward changing public or institutional decision-making processes. *Social justice* focuses on inequality in rights, resources, processes, and treatments and on valuing equality among all groups. Individuals, communities, and institutions can make change.[3] *Volunteering* is like activism in many ways in that people spend their time in service of others, but in this book, I only consider it activism if it focuses on making change. Cleaning litter from a stream is volunteering; advocating to change littering laws is activism.

Here I use the term activism but with the assumption that your activism may be related to changing the government through advocacy or ensuring fair treatment through social justice. Or something uniquely yours.

What Type of Activist Are You?

Three types of activists can use *What's On Your Sign?* First, the *unexpected activist,* who makes a sudden decision to get into activism and doesn't know how to start. Have you confronted a situation that led you to want to join the fight? You are an unexpected activist.

The *unproductive activist* has been involved in activism but isn't sure whether their work is making a difference. If you are already working in a cause but wonder if you could be more productive, use the tools in this book to check your impact and connect with an organization that helps you grow.

Finally, this book is for the *untested activist,* who is clear about the change they want to see but hasn't begun. An example of an untested activist is a teen who knows their cause and is ready to start the work. Another example is an empty-nester who hasn't had much time for the cause but now can focus on activism.

My Story: The Unexpected Activist

I am an unexpected activist. I'm not the only one. Reactions to an unqualified male candidate beating a qualified female candidate may have varied, but many citizens were in mourning in 2016. Psych Central reported on the day after the election traffic to the *5 Stages of Grief and Loss* page was up 210%.[4]

I spent one glorious day in Washington, DC, at the Women's March and saw I wasn't the only unexpected activist. In the words of Ilana

Glazer, "I had never seen so many angry, progressive, white people."[5] After the March I called my elected representatives so often I recognized the aides' voices. The ache in my chest had subsided by February and, although I was still scared, I felt as if the palpable joy and energy of the Women's March had healed my heart a bit. I was lurching around trying to get up to speed on activism and spreading my time in a scatter-shot fashion.

To educate myself I attended a Gamaliel community organizing workshop. President Barack Obama began his community organizing career at Gamaliel; their mission is "to empower ordinary people to effectively participate in the political, environmental, social and economic decisions affecting their lives."[6] My workshop facilitators shared personal activism stories with palpable passion even after decades of doing the work. The secret of why they were still successful? They had chosen a cause that made them angry. Gut-wrenchingly angry. Because activism is stressful and at times not particularly fruitful, their advice was to pick the issue that makes you angry and keeps you going.

It seemed natural for many of the attendees, who already knew what made them angry. The fellow next to me walked a grocery store picket line as a preschooler. But I sensed many participants were having difficulty finding their gut-wrenching issue. Should we pick our congressional representative who called us losers because we wrote letters and called to express our views? What about our senators, both Republicans with purses filled with money from wealthy donors and lobbyists? Those issues angered me, but I still didn't know what got me square in the gut.

On Sunday, the third day of the workshop, I received a devastating text—my mother had a stroke, and in the words of my brother, "it's bad." I left the Gamaliel training for North Carolina to be with my mother, as did my other brothers. Gathered in a circle in the hospital waiting room, my brothers and I made the difficult decision to withhold treatment and put her in hospice. Despite my fretting as a child, she had lived to be 94 years old and managed to take the shuttle from her assisted living facility to vote for Trump just months before her stroke.

Several months later I emerged from my grief and started again with the process of "what makes me angry?" I figured if I had found the right cause my mother's death wouldn't have sidetracked me. The lesson the Gamaliel staff taught me—your passion will get you through the tough times.

Changing tactics, I decided to start from scratch and examine my life focus. I have about 25 years of active energy to devote to a cause. I chose to find out what matters and where I want to spend my precious time. And in the process, I found my passion in an unexpected place.

It takes time and energy to examine your life in this way. My effort allowed me to focus on activism, but also affected my life positively in countless ways; it's a significant payoff for the effort. And if you can focus on your passion, you will have an impact on others. Your passion and activism are integral parts of you as a person, and your success may improve the lives of others, including those you love.

There are many opportunities to make an impact through activism. In fact, there is competition among causes for good activists, and these organizations want to attract passionate and motivated individuals. This excellent situation means you have choices and opportunities.

All you unexpected activists—are you saying to yourself, "But wait, I'm not a real activist"? You are. We are all activists. If you look back at your life, you can name times when you have used your knowledge, skills, and influence to try to make a difference.

Have you ever marched into the principal's office to advocate for a change at your child's school? What about asking a friend to avoid using a word with racial connotations? Everyone starts somewhere and sometime to make a change.

Many of us have been free riders in social change; people who enjoy the ride but let others pay the cost. We must resist. As Dolly says, we must be brave enough to try.

Talia's Story: The Unproductive Activist

Talia, a loan officer, finishes her final loan for the day. This one is particularly satisfying because the member, a divorced mom of three children, has struggled. A few years ago, the credit union gave her a Fresh Start loan to buy a reliable used car. These loans are for those with poor credit and carry a high interest rate. But she paid each month and now has decent enough credit to refinance at a better rate. The money she saves each month will put her much closer to financial peace.

Talia enjoys her job as a loan officer for just this reason—helping families get their financial house in order. She sees the positive difference this makes, not only in paying their bills but also in their self-esteem and mental health. Her day may be long, but she leaves with a good feeling. She heads to her car and sees Tammy pulling out. "I'll see you at the college," Tammy yells out her car window and waves goodbye. Talia, Tammy, and several others from the credit union are heading to the local community college to encourage students to register to vote. Tammy asked Talia to help with this program more than 10 years ago and although Talia believes it's crucial to vote she's not inspired by the work. These kids are much like her own boys—they rebel against listening to their parents about registering but will readily listen to a stranger. She likes the other volunteers and the students but is curious if all this time and effort makes a difference. She wonders if she is selfish to want more interesting, exciting, and impactful activism.

Talia turns 40 this year and is readying for the time when her last child is out on his own. This will free her up for other activities. Although she can work more hours or enjoy leisure time, she feels ready to step up and focus on making her community a better place. She's not sure her past efforts have made much of a difference.

Talia is one of the many individuals in the world who wish to make a change but are unsure if they are having an impact. You will follow Talia's story throughout the book as she moves from being an unproductive activist to pursuing her passion and making the change she wants to see in the world.

Brenda's Story: The Untested Activist

Brenda trudges through her paper-strewn high school hall, fingering her car keys. Poised at the exit door is Officer Holly, whose short, spiked hair gives a pixie vibe. Beaming at Brenda, she says, "Turn that frown upside down!" Brenda makes a half-hearted stab at a grin. That makes her laugh, and Officer Holly reaches up to give her a high five.

"Did you make it to work on time yesterday?" Officer Holly inquires.

"I did, thanks to you and your handy car-thief tool."

"Police officers know all the bad-guy tricks. I'm glad I could help you get your keys out of your car."

When Brenda was in middle school, a teen came on campus and shot a student. Since then the school system has ramped up safety procedures for entering campuses and stationed a police officer at every school. Brantley High School lucked out with Officer Holly. Although her perpetually upbeat demeanor is grating at times, particularly at the crack of dawn, she has become part of the fabric of the Brantley community.

The day of the shooting Brenda was on a different side of the middle school campus, but she heard what sounded like a pop. She didn't pay attention until she saw teachers running in that direction. Her best friend Callie ran in to tell her it was a shooting. "Mark – from our homeroom last year? You know, that guy that fell asleep most days?

Some guy came onto campus and got into an argument with him. He shot Mark!"

Mark survived. But Brenda's sense of safety didn't.

Now the school has a different vibe. Brenda wishes the school board could see the watchful teachers in the halls during class changes. The routine lock-down drills. Officer Holly in the cafeteria, eating her tiny salad, chatting with students, a gun on her hip. Brenda feels as if her heart is going to expand inside her until it explodes.

Last month in her English class Mrs. Hughes assigned a persuasive essay. In honor of the students who survived the massacre at Marjory Stoneman Douglas High School in Parkland, Florida, Brenda barreled through her piece on school safety.

> *Why we need Officer Holly at Brantley High School*
> *By Brenda Atterman*
> *Officer Holly was assigned to Brantley High School to keep us safe from school shootings. She does not keep us safe from guns, but she is vital to our school.*
>
> *Although I trust that Officer Holly would give her life protecting me from a gun, the chances of a school shooting happening, or if one does, her stopping it, are slim to none. The 2013 Congressional Research Service report on law enforcement officers in schools questioned whether schools need police since they are a safe place for teachers and students.*[7]
>
> *Even though there was a law enforcement officer at Stoneman Douglas High School in Parkland, Florida, 17 people were murdered. The school officer did not enter the building during the shooting. How*

likely is it that an officer will be at the spot where a shooter takes out a gun? And if they are, what are the chances they can stop the shooting?

The Congressional Research Service report tells us there are no answers to those questions. They don't know if school officers keep students safe from guns. Instead, the authors say that schools should create a comprehensive safety plan that includes all aspects of school safety, such as bullying prevention, mediation, mental health programs, and security equipment. Only if the assessment shows a need should a school hire a police officer. According to Psychology Today, "The rationale for additional, proactive, preventive measures is well worth repeating: when a student enters a school with a gun, and an intent to kill, it's already too late."[8]

So, Officer Holly isn't going to keep me safe from guns. But we need to keep her anyway, because of what she does for the other students and me.

She is always watching, so she notices signs of physical abuse and intervenes.

She runs incredible self-defense classes after school.

Yesterday I saw her helping a teacher corral an out-of-control student. She didn't body slam or use handcuffs. She used a convincing voice and a big smile.

She shows up, and cheers for everyone at our Talent Shows even though she is off duty.

She gives stern but loving talking-tos to male students who start to get grabby with females.

She directs traffic in the morning and after school, so teachers and students have one less aggravation to deal with.

> *I often see students pull her aside. I don't know what they are talking about, but she listens with her entire body. That means a lot to us.*
>
> *Kids are super-good at hiding what is going on inside. So, when you accidentally bump someone in the hall, and they call you an a**hole, it might be that bump 'broke the camel's back' for that person. Officer Holly shows us that getting to know students helps solve those problems before they escalate to violence.*
>
> *Personally, I feel that although Officer Holly was assigned here because of a school shooting, she has become a part of our school community. She makes students feel positive about police officers, she makes us feel safe in ways other than what the school board intended, and she helps students and teachers focus on learning. Guns need to be controlled, but please let us keep Officer Holly.*

Mrs. Hughes didn't give her a perfect score because she never gives anyone a perfect score, but Brenda received a 97 and a message, "I can sense from your writing how much passion you have for this issue. What are you going to do about it?" Brenda thinks about it a lot. "What am I going to do about it?"

How to Use What's On Your Sign?

I used to struggle with the magnitude of needs in my world, bombarded by the targeted asks and volunteer fundraisers and charitable organizations looking for help. Instead of diving in, I wanted to remember the value of my time and use it efficiently and effectively. This led me to research effective activism. I want my activism to make a real difference.

I encourage you to read the entire book because it will improve your odds of making a match of your passions and gifts with your opportunities for activism. If you decide to omit some sections, still complete the objective for each chapter.

If you have limited time, here are the suggestions for chapters to complete based on the type of activist you most resemble.

Unexpected Activist

If you are an unexpected activist, you should read the entire book to determine your focus, understand your gifts, find great opportunities, and maximize your performance. But if you have time limits, I recommend Part 1: Your Passion and Part 2: Your Gifts.

Untested Activist

If you are an untested activist and are clear about your passion, read Part 2: Your Gifts, Part 3: Your Activism Options, Part 4: Your Activism Choice, and Part 5: Your Passion in Action.

Unproductive Activist

If you are an unproductive activist and feel good about your passion and gifts, read Part 3: Your Activism Options, Part 4: Your Activism Choice, and Part 5: Your Passion in Action.

The What's On Your Sign? Workbook

The *What's On Your Sign? Workbook* is a companion to *What's On Your Sign? How to Focus your Passion and Change the World,* with practical tools to help you get started in activism.

The WOYS? Workbook is designed to help you complete the activism path described here. Each chapter in *What's On Your Sign?* has a corresponding chapter in *The WOYS? Workbook.*

You will see a note in *What's On Your Sign?* like the one below when it is time to go to *The WOYS? Workbook* and complete the corresponding resource.

Go to Chapter 1 in *The WOYS? Workbook*

For chapter 1, go to *The WOYS? Workbook* to complete the survey "What kind of activist are you?"

Other resources in *The WOYS? Workbook* include worksheets, reflections, and checklists to guide you on your activism path.

Chapter Summary

In Chapter 1 of *What's On Your Sign?* I delve into my activism journey, explaining how I came to be an unexpected activist following the 2016 election. I read every book I could lay my hands on to help me focus my efforts and move confidently into activism work but did not find a book that gave me the direction and confidence I wanted. My social concerns are varied and broad, and no one book helped me focus on the best match for my skills and passions.

So I reviewed research, books, and other sources and put together a process that incorporates research results and best practices. The result is *What's On Your Sign?* and *The WOYS? Workbook*. The methods described in my books helped me focus my passion and change the world, and I hope they do the same for you.

I am an unexpected activist, tossed into activism by world events, Talia has been working on a cause but wonders if she is making a difference, and Brenda wants to transform a terrible experience into a safer world. Although we are distinct types of activists, *What's On Your Sign?* contains the tools and inspiration we need

CHAPTER 2

Find Your Passion

Before you tell your life what you intend to do with it, listen for what it intends to do with you. Before you tell your life what truths and values you have decided to live up to, let your life tell you what truths you embody, what values you represent. ~ Parker Palmer[9]

Objective

Create a vision of the change you want in the world.

Goal

List three to five activism passions from your vision of the change you want in the world.

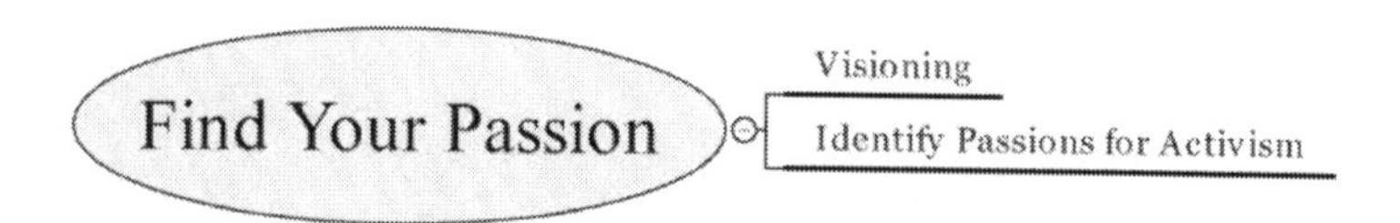

TO FIND YOUR PASSIONS, create a vision of your ideal life and world. Then look for the gaps between your ideal world and your life right now. The gaps between what you see as ideal and what should change are where you find your passions for activism.

My friend Catherine invited me to a work party at the Great Smoky Mountain Peace Pagoda in Newport, Tennessee. She admired the resident Monks and often helped with the erection of the magnificent structure. So, we made the dangerous trip up a remote mountain. I was not sure what to expect, but I learned about the power of a vision.

Brother Utsumi's Story

The Great Smoky Mountains Peace Pagoda is the vision of Buddhist Monk Brother Utsumi, who came to the United States from Japan to protest nuclear weapons and promote peace. Brother Utsumi's passion is abolishing nuclear weapons, and one way he does his work is by building a gigantic concrete peace pagoda on a remote Tennessee mountaintop about a two-hour drive from the nuclear facility at Oak Ridge.

Brother Utsumi, Sister Denise, and many volunteers erect the peace pagoda; the work has taken several years and will need five more. My friend Catherine and I traveled up the mountain for a fall work party. The final path requires 4-wheel drive, so Sister Denise, sporting concrete-splattered glasses, hauled us up in her truck, dropped us off at the temple, then ran the rest of the way up the hill to continue pouring concrete. All sorts of people contributed to the vision while we were there—a graduate student from Virginia, a Dutch citizen who travels to the U.S. for work parties each year, a transgender woman, a senior citizen, a Presbyterian minister and his daughter, and a Buddhist monk from Massachusetts.

Brother Utsumi's vision of a Peace Pagoda in a remote area in the Bible Belt shows the power of a big idea for change. He and Sister Denise remind me of the power of dreaming big, having faith in people, and keeping your passion over the long haul.

Visioning

There are many opportunities to serve and make a change. But before you jump into the fray, take time for visioning. With a clear passion, you have the opportunity for more in-depth engagement developed over time; it won't disappear when a new cause challenges your attention.

Visioning means drawing yourself from the present and into the future. To develop your vision, you can use one or more techniques, whatever suits your preferences and frees your mind.

I used focusing questions to create my vision of an ideal life and world. But other visioning techniques focus on more creative and less rational approaches than mine. In her book, *Visioning*, Lucia Capacchione provides creative options such as meditation, visual research using magazine and picture collections, collage-making, and wordplay (which is, literally, playing with words).[10] Another creative technique is mind-mapping, in which you use a visual representation of your ideas combined with a tool to relate, reorganize, and rearrange, resulting in improved creativity.[11] In mind-mapping, put the big idea in the middle of the map. Using spokes, add refining elements to the main idea. Mind-mapping mimics how the brain processes information.[12]

Here is a sample mind map:

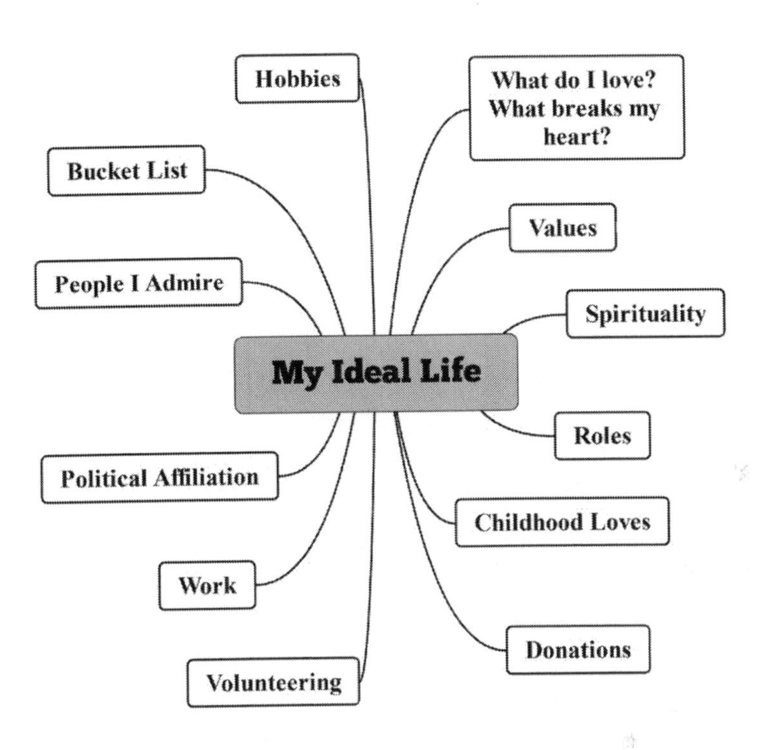

A mind-map might be the perfect way to free your mind to imagine your future. But go with your flow and use the visioning technique or combination of techniques that serve you best.

Topics for Visioning

Being an activist means doing your best to make a difference; recognizing your passion supports change. Start with a vision of your ideal life and world.

To best understand your passions, you will:

~ Create a vision for your ideal life
~ Create a vision for your ideal world
~ Identify your passions

Your Ideal Life

To create a vision for your ideal life, you will examine the roles you play, the experiences you want, your values, and learnings from your past.

Your Roles

Being an activist is only one role you play in life. You may also be a spouse, parent, employee, house cleaner, cook, lawn mower, and caregiver. Having a distinct focus will help you fulfill the essential roles and rid yourself of those not part of your vision.

Make a list of the roles you play in life. You'll come up with dozens.

Here's the kicker. We can't handle more than five roles well. Most of us are trying to juggle many instead of staying focused on a few important ones. For example, I can try to keep my house clean, organized, and stocked with the household goods we need. That's a great idea. But what if I clean at the expense of other more important roles, such as being a parent? Is a tidy living room more important than spending time with my child?

Create your list of roles and then narrow it to the five you believe are most worthy of your focus.

Go to Chapter 2 in *The WOYS? Workbook*

Your Bucket List

How do *wants* relate to making a difference? I'm asking you to look for inspiration on your bucket list, the activities you want to do before you die ("kick the bucket"). Your bucket list holds items with no relationship to activism. But bear with me, because your bucket list is integral to finding your activism passion.

Your bucket list has experiences that matter to you. In fact, they matter so much you are saying they are essential to your life experiences. You are motivated and passionate – so use them in your activism.

Bucket lists are useful because they have goals. Bucket list items tend to be difficult and specific.[13] Rather than vague wishes such as "Before I die I'd like to travel," bucket lists have vivid and concrete goals like, "Before I die, I will travel to Paris, sit in cafes and people-watch, take pictures from the top of the Eiffel Tower, then follow the Tour de France from start to finish."

I include a bucket list in the visioning work because your bucket list focuses on wants, not shoulds, and the items motivate you.

Plus, there are ways to incorporate your bucket list into your activism. Is there something on your bucket list you can include in your activism? For example, if you have bungee jumping on your bucket list, brainstorm ways you can use it for your cause. Get sponsors for your jump; it will motivate you.

Go to Chapter 2 in *The WOYS? Workbook*

Your Values

Start with your values. Your values are the driving force of your life, and it is essential to make sure you are following the important ones.

Examples of values are self-respect, quality of life, family, generosity, and courage. Once you have named the values most important to you, change them into I-statements.

~ I have self-respect.
~ I enjoy an excellent quality of life.
~ I love my family.
~ I am generous with others.
~ I face difficult circumstances with courage.

Those statements are part of your ideal life. Now design your vision of yourself living your ideal life.

Now bring together your reflections on the elements of an ideal life. Write your Ideal Life Vision.

Go to Chapter 2 in *The WOYS? Workbook*

Learning From Your Past

Look back at your life experiences and the people you've met. Learn from those experiences to help guide your life as you move forward.

Choices

What meaningful choices did you make in your life and why did you make them? What would you do differently and how does this help you look to the future? They say we learn more from our mistakes than from our successes. How can learning from your mistakes inform your future?

When I reflected on this question, I realized I have always shied away from conflict. Sometimes it serves me well, but my unwillingness to speak up when I saw injustice makes me ashamed. This learning informs my life and particularly my activism.

Dreams

As children, we are free to imagine our future without the burdens of being an adult. When you were a child, what did you envision as your future? What did you want to be when you grew up? How might this change your future focus?

Growing up with a bunch of brothers made me an athletic child who felt free to move about the world without my gender getting in the way. As I absorbed society's messages about what girls should and shouldn't do, I felt less free. Girls should wear dresses. Girls shouldn't play with trucks. I still struggle but try to find ways to break free from society's expectations of the female role.

People

You've met many people in your life. Celebrities in the arts, entertainment, government, business, sports, and activism have affected you. Who do you admire and want to emulate?

When I think of those I admire I realize they are no-nonsense, get-the-job-done types. People who are willing to speak up and say the emperor has no clothes. Sometimes, when I hesitate to speak up, I picture them to help me be brave.

Go to Chapter 2 in *The WOYS? Workbook*

How You Make Change

The best predictor of future behavior is past behavior. Unless you have a momentous change of focus, you tend to behave the same way as you go through life. Examine the ways you have made change. You may choose to continue to do the same methods that have worked well for you. Or this may tell you what you need to change in the future to meet your goals.

You offer time, which is the hours you give. Your talent is those skills you donate. Finally, treasure is financial support you provide.

~ Consider your time – the hours you have spent supporting causes. What activism causes have you helped? Where have you volunteered?
~ Consider your talent – the skills you have used to support causes. What talents have you used in activism and volunteering?
~ Finally, consider your treasure – where have you directed money to a cause?

Now, look at your political and religious preferences.

- What is your political affiliation? How has it affected your activism or volunteering?
- What are your religious tenets or principles? How have they affected your activism or volunteering?

Are you still invested in the choices you made in the past, or do you need to change to meet your goals?

Callings

Author Tara Mohr has a chapter in her book *Playing Big* on your calling and how to recognize it. She defines calling as, "...a longing to address a particular need or problem in the world." [14] Calling has a religious connotation to me, but her definition sums up the idea of activism well. Here are her ways to recognize a calling:

> *"You feel an unusually vivid pain or frustration around the status quo of a particular issue. You see a powerful vision - vague or clear - about what could be around some aspect of the status quo. That vision keeps coming back into your mind and keeps tugging at your heart. You feel huge resistance. A part of you wants to run in the other direction. You feel a sense of "this work is mine to do" or of having received an assignment to do a particular piece of work in the world."* [15]

Parker Palmer, whose beautiful words are at the beginning of this chapter, calls this concept vocation,

> *"This is something I can't not do, for reasons I'm unable to explain to anyone else and don't fully understand myself but are nonetheless completing."* [16]

Is there anything in your life that affects you this way? Something powerful that draws you even though you feel resistance to it? Pay close attention, because it may be a calling.

Go to Chapter 2 in *The WOYS? Workbook*

Your Ideal Life Vision

In 1988 I attended a Day Planner seminar at work sponsored by the Franklin Institute. I enjoyed naming my values and creating a vision of my future self to help me focus my life on what is important to me. Perhaps it was my workplace's way of forcing productivity, but I took to the process with ease.

Now, 30 years later, I wouldn't change anything about my vision or values. That's remarkable and speaks to being sure of my values, which are steadfast in my life. The vision doesn't talk about the how of living my life, just the focus and the ideal. It is the place to start activities in my life including my service to the world. I will admit I have not yet become my ideal self, but I stay focused on growing closer to it.

If you have not done this kind of reflecting, I encourage you to. It's time-consuming but understanding your ideal vision of yourself pays off in many ways. It guides all aspects of your life, including your activism.

Think of yourself in the future, 5, 10, or maybe 15 years from now. What do you see? Describe yourself living your ideal life through the roles and values vital for you.

Here is an example of a Life Vision, based on values. Notice that this does not describe the "how" of the vision but just what "is."

I love and enjoy my family and friends. I have compassion for myself and others. My passion for art is part of all areas of my life – my environment, my career, and my activism. I live a life of honesty and integrity.

Go to Chapter 2 in *The WOYS? Workbook*

Use the work you've done in this chapter, particularly on your values, to envision your ideal life.

Your Ideal World

I suspect since you are reading this book, you want to change the world. When you reflect on the state of your community, the country, or the world, what do you wish? What is your ideal vision?

Describe your ideal world if you were master of the universe. How would you include these factors in your perfect world? In the following chart are examples.

Factor	Example
Relationships	"People follow a moral code of conduct."
Education	"Education is valued, well-funded, and free for everyone."
Government	"Government supports only necessary functions."
Currency	"Currency is worldwide and electronic."

Go to Chapter 2 in *The WOYS? Workbook*

Your Current World

Now reflect on your current world and compare it to your ideal vision. Where is change necessary to get to your ideal world? For example, if you imagined a perfect world with no weapons, what would need to change?

What makes you angry?

The Gamaliel facilitators taught me the importance of drawing on anger as a vision source. Although dwelling on anger is uncomfortable, I use my passion to keep me steadfast even in trying times.

What makes you angry? What gives you that feeling in your gut? What disgusts you so much you must turn away? What inspires you and makes you want to act?

What do you love?

Love is the key to the passion you choose for your activism. Rex Burkholder describes the reasons he got involved in activism in his deteriorated Portland, Oregon, community, eventually serving in government, focusing on ecological issues. "Why would ordinary people put on bright orange vests, walk the night streets carrying only flashlights, and confront young men most likely armed with guns? The only answer I can come up with is love."[17] He loved his neighborhood and the people in it, and this led to a many-decades focus that transformed his town.

When you recall your childhood when your imagination was free to go places without having to weigh the expectations of others, what did you love? Can you reawaken that love?

Heartbreak is the hard side of love. What has broken your heart? What makes you sad or ashamed?

Go to Chapter 2 in *The WOYS? Workbook*

Your Passion for Change

When you complete the visioning, find three to five passions in your life to inform your activism choices.

If you find gaps between your ideal and the current world, these are perfect places to explore. Another method is looking for themes in your visioning. For example, you see a thread throughout your visioning – you tend to focus on homelessness. When you were a child, you did chores to earn money and donated to the local shelter. Now you knit scarves and hats for the firefighter's campaign to give to the community. Homelessness is a theme and a passion.

Go to Chapter 2 in *The WOYS? Workbook*

Talia's Story

Talia's Ideal Life

Talia had never written a Life Plan, although she was able to describe a vision of her future life. Using a collage visioning technique, she started a "vision board" to capture her wishes for the future.

Talia started cutting words and pictures out of magazines. If they sparked her interest, they made the "cut." She then glued them into clusters on her vision board. She hung her vision board above her desk for inspiration.

From the vision of herself, she realized the importance of her family. Images of families playing together, and words like 'love' and 'relating' pepper her board. This helps her see where she wasn't prioritizing some roles in her life. For example, after a day at work, she lounged for hours in front of the TV to decompress. And calling this time with her spouse didn't really cut it since they didn't talk much to each other.

She also sees words and phrases like 'boldness,' 'wake up,' and 'dreaming into doing,' which she sees as a yearning for change.

Vision for My Life

Talia's vision of herself in the future is:

My family loves me and enjoys me. I have a network of friends. I travel and learn new things. I make the world a better place. I feel good. I have no regrets about things left undone. I'm at peace. I have enough money, so I don't need to worry. My husband and I enjoy our free time together. We have expressed our affection and care for one another. Our children respect us. They see us as worthy role models. They rely on our advice. We love them unconditionally.

Talia's values are:

I love my family.
I am physically healthy.
I positively impact others.
I am productive.
I am content.

What roles are important in your life?

Mother, spouse, provider, helper, learner.

What roles did you want that you have not yet played?

Talia added Activist to her role list because of the need for everyone to ramp up their contributions to making the world a better place.

What did you want to be when you grew up?

Talia dreamed of working as an animal care technician. It was the only career she ever considered as a child.

Who do you admire and want to emulate?

The celebrity Talia most admires is Dolly Parton because she invests in the local community to create jobs and her book program helps children. Talia wants to have that kind of impact on the world.

The friend Talia most admires is Cathy. Talia used to know Cathy by another name, but in the past few years Cathy has transitioned and is living the gender identity she has always felt was her true self. Cathy's bravery in living the life she wants despite the danger awes Talia.

Talia recognizes that, unlike Cathy, she is a people-pleaser and it sometimes leads to her suppressing her feelings and ideas.

Talia's Bucket List

Talia didn't have a bucket list, so this was a fun exercise for her. Talia's husband Mark created his bucket list, too. Talia's list has:

~ hike in all the national parks
~ travel to Italy
~ lend money to women with children
~ reach her ideal weight
~ learn to ballroom dance and then take a cruise so she can show off her new skills
~ see a Broadway musical with a big star

Sadly, there wasn't much overlap of Talia's list with Mark's. He doesn't enjoy hiking. But he agreed to do dance lessons and take a cruise with Talia.

She loved the idea of being clear about her values and recognized they were the same as when she was younger. But she hadn't made a conscious choice to focus her precious time on those values and make sure they guided her life.

Although her vision doesn't speak to the "hows" of living her life, just the focus and the ideal, Talia was able to list to-do items from the exercise. For example, to support her values of loving her family, she wants to try to interact with them using more positives than negatives. To help her value of positively affecting others, she wants to make her activism more productive. Finally, to support her bucket list item of learning to ballroom dance, she and Mark signed up for dance lessons.

Talia's learnings from her past

Talia thought about the crucial choices she has made in her life, and why she made them. This helped her analyze what she would do differently in the future.

Talia changed majors in college even though she wanted to work with animals. Her goal from childhood was to become an animal care technician. She loves animals, rescues her pets, and loves taking them for walks in any weather. After a disastrous first quarter in college, she was pretty sure she'd derailed any plan to go into a healthcare field. Exploring foundation courses in college led her to change her major to business instead.

She's glad she found a credit union for her career because of the way they care for members. But she doesn't like being inside all day.

Talia has a keen sense of making the world a better place through her work, which is indeed a blessing. Because she helps families with their finances, they improve themselves and potentially their future. Working for a non-profit makes her proud. She likes the idea of the credit union as a non-profit cooperative that serves members, not customers. And they focus on developing financial capability.

She linked the credit union staff with community organizations needing help. For example, one group offers emergency aid to residents, and the credit union delivered financial capability classes. In her work, she sees how power differences affect financial capability.

Talia would have worried about money less, and this informs her future by reminding her to follow her passion.

She wishes she had cared less about what other people thought of her. This informs her choices for the future because she will remind herself to get out of her comfort zone. She wants to say "rubbish" more.

Talia was always looking forward and not celebrating her accomplishments. In the future, she will remind herself of what she is doing for her cause.

She wishes she had spoken up more about injustice. She is already taking steps to understand what she wants to do in the future and trying to get out of her comfort zone. She will educate herself and prepare to deal with potential issues and how she can solve them.

Talia believes to achieve her life plan she will need to stay focused on what is important to her. With a limited amount of time each day she wants to make positive choices. She decided to give up TV for 30 days to allow more time for service and her family.

Talia's Ideal World

Talia's description of her ideal world is:

> *My world is peaceful. We know how to relate to one another. There are no borders. Our environment is thriving. We appreciate differences in each other. Wanting things is rare. We take care of everyone's basic needs. We eat plants instead of animals. Everyone has justice. Universal design means the world works for everyone - able-bodied or not.*

Talia's Current World

Talia lists the issues that break her heart:

- Violence and mistreatment toward anyone or anything helpless, such as kids and sexual assault victims
- The impact of global warming on everyone, particularly on countries who didn't cause the problem in the first place
- Lack of financial capability and the effect on the person and their family, particularly women
- Racism, particularly the impact on children

Talia gets angry about these issues:

- Domestic violence and abuse
- Bullying
- Sexual assault
- Exploitation of our Earth

What/who needs Talia's help:

- Families, particularly women, who are struggling financially
- Nature, the planet, the town, and the national parks

Talia sees the gaps between her vision of an ideal world and the current world. One is income inequality. She also sees that we don't appreciate each other's differences, which shows in the mistreatment of those with less power and protection of privilege. Finally, she worries about the health of the environment.

How Talia makes change

Over the years, Talia ended up doing a lot of hodgepodge volunteer work. She helped build houses for Habitat for Humanity. After her children were born, people roped her into a lot of volunteering, such as chaperoning field trips, and she was the unofficial school nurse. She felt satisfied with these volunteer roles, but she wasn't passionate about them. Still, they held clues to her strengths and interests, as well as less motivating areas.

Her first long-term, formal volunteer position was as a community mediator for unmarried parents with kids. This work involved encouraging the parents to stay focused on the best interests of the child and helping them reach an agreement they were both happy with rather than letting a judge decide for them. Most of these family situations were ugly, but Talia felt pleased to mediate a settlement that worked for them and the child.

She saw many power differentials here - between the parents and, of course, for the child. One of her learnings from her training for this volunteer job was the need to model equality for the clients. Mediators worked in pairs, and they stayed attentive to the power dynamics of their work together.

Talia and her husband found a liberal church community focused on social justice. Through Unitarian Universalism, she has been able to release the religious dogma from her childhood, which opened her mind to a variety of religions and other spiritual sources to inform her path. Of course, if you join a church you end up volunteering, so she took on various roles, such as teaching religious education classes.

Talia and her husband donated to their church but otherwise mostly just gave when people asked.

Talia always felt uninformed and disconnected from politics because she didn't align to a party. This confused her and led to less interest in political issues. After the 2016 election, she educated herself and found that she aligns with several political platforms.

Talia's Passion for Change

Talia does not believe she has a calling, but she found the process of reflection and visioning valuable for finding themes in her life.

Talia's passions are for vulnerable women, animals, and the environment.

She sees the gaps between her vision of an ideal world and the current world as income inequality, mistreatment of those with less privilege, and global warming.

Chapter Summary

There are many opportunities to serve and make a change. However, before you jump into the fray, take time for visioning to be clear about what you want from your life and what change you want in the world. The visioning will help you identify your passions and prepare you to be a more effective activist.

In Chapter 2 you create a vision for an ideal life and world, using methods such as worksheets, mind-mapping, and vision boards to clarify your roles, wants, and values.

You describe your ideal world, reflecting on subjects such as equality, justice, and education. Next, you recognize how the world is now and use your image of an ideal life to focus your passions.

This reflection clarifies your most important roles, the people you admire, unfulfilled dreams, and your bucket list. Your vision of an ideal life is the first step on the What's On Your Sign? path. With your ideal society in mind, you reflect on what change you want to make in the world.

The story of Brother Utsumi shows the power and persistence of a big vision that stays steadfast and keeps him focused. He has a clear idea of the ideal world and what change he wants to make.

Talia is moving from being an unproductive activist to refining and clarifying the currents of her life into a direction for change.

I hope you found the resources you needed to identify three to five activism passions. In the next chapter, you will begin the process of identifying the gifts you bring to activism.

Activist in Action: Rhonda Lynn Rucker

Choosing a method for activism is probably similar to choosing your vocation—your work should be the point at which your talents meet the needs of the world. –Rhonda R. Rucker

Why did you choose your activism cause?

That's difficult to answer since I don't have just one activism cause. One of my primary concerns, however, is the environment. As a child, I loved reading about animals and plants and how they were all connected in a web of interdependency. These were the days of DDT and its threat to the bald eagle and other large predatory birds. Then the Endangered Species Act was passed, and the numbers of the eagles rebounded—one of the major success stories in the environmental movement.

However, science has now shown that the ecological situation is so much more complex than we understood in those days. With climate change, habitat destruction, loss of biodiversity, and so many other perils, the stakes are incredibly higher.

In fact, the more I learn about the damage we're doing to this Earth, the more I realize that nothing else may matter. We might not only send other species into extinction, we might send ourselves as well. And if we don't, we will make this world into a living hell, where we fight over disappearing resources, land, and food. That's why I think it's imperative for us to get serious about putting the Earth first. After all, it's our only home.

How did you decide what method to use for your activism?

Choosing a method for activism is probably similar to choosing your vocation—your work should be the point at which your talents meet the needs of the world. My husband and I are folk musicians. Our performances also include plenty of storytelling and history. Much of folk music was originally protest music, and my husband started his career by singing in the civil rights movement.

History should always inform our choices for the future; otherwise, we repeat the same mistakes. One of the things we try to do is teach people about past events. Some of these stories are really inspiring, and they show the power people have when they band together.

I am also an author, so I use that platform to spread these same messages. Reading *The Grapes of Wrath* as a teenager taught me how persuasive novels can be.

Were there areas where you felt unprepared for your work?

It took me several years of performing before I really felt comfortable or "prepared" to use our presentations as a vehicle for activism. But nowadays it comes naturally to me.

What advice do you have for new activists?

First of all, don't wait until you feel like you are "ready" or "prepared" like I did. Just take the plunge and do it. You are as qualified as anyone else, and you are certainly entitled to an opinion.

Secondly, I think it's a great strength to not be wedded to one particular cause. So often, many of these issues are tied together and affect one another. Whenever possible, work with others on their goals. Too often, we focus on our differences and we're unwilling to compromise. Then nothing gets done. Instead of helping one another, we form circular firing squads. Whenever possible, we need to search for common ground, understand the concerns of others, and give them a helping hand. It's an imperfect, diverse world, and if we hold back our support because of petty differences, we'll create a dysfunctional world.

Rhonda Rucker is a physician, musician, author, teacher, and storyteller. She and her husband, James "Sparky" Rucker perform around the world. For more information about Rhonda's work go to www.sparkyandrhonda.com.

PART 2

Your Gifts

In Part 2 focus on your gifts. Understanding your gifts helps you decide where you fit best in activism. Pinpoint the skills and knowledge you can apply right now. Look at your motivation for activism so you can make the best match for your work.

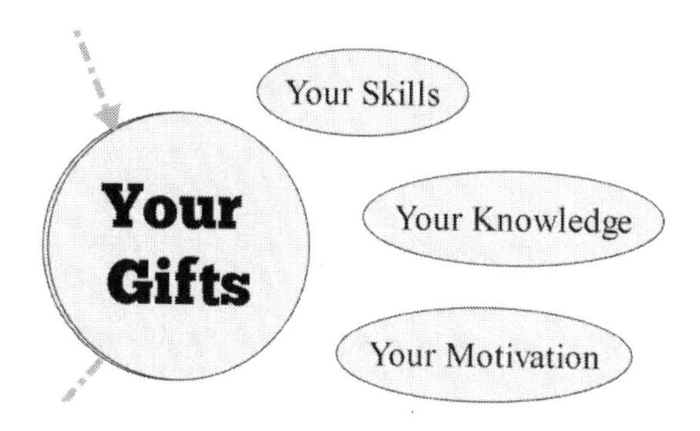

Part 2 includes:

Chapter 3: Identify Your Skills

Chapter 4: Inventory Your Knowledge

Chapter 5: Be Clear About Your Motivation

CHAPTER 3

Identify Your Gifts

Movements teach you to make plans and then remake them on the go. This is one of the reasons why artists have always been so essential to America's freedom movements. Any artist will tell you that you can't become proficient in art without careful attention to the masters. You have to know your history, practice the moves of those who have gone before you, and make their music your own. But you haven't mastered the art until you've learned to improvise - to take the wisdom passed down to you and write the next verse of humanity's collective song. ~Reverend Dr. William J. Barber, II [18]

Objective

Identify your activism skills and other skills you can apply to activism.

Goal

List three to five skills you can apply to activism right now.

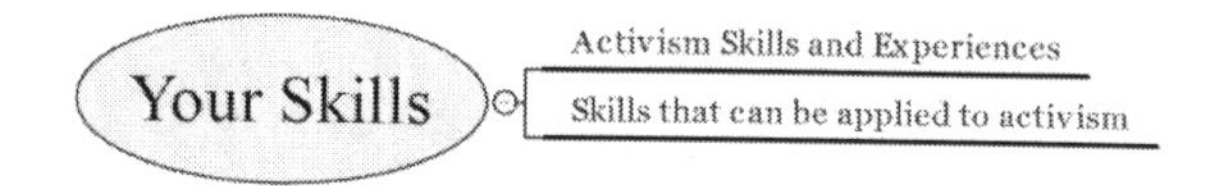

IN THE LAST CHAPTER, you worked on your activism focus and hopefully found several passions in your reflections to inform your direction. In this chapter, you will focus on the skills and experiences you bring to activism and pinpoint what you can translate to activism work.

Your Skills

Because there are many ways to make change, match your skills to your activism. This is an important starting point because you are motivated and have the skills to begin.

Your Personal Skills

I admire professional activists because it is not easy or lucrative work. But most activists are volunteers. You are doing this in addition to the other roles in your life as a partner, employee, parent, or caregiver. You may not have the advantage of the training and internships available to professional activists.

First, gather information that documents your skills. This might include your resumé, performance appraisals, or surveys. These are great reminders of your experience and skills. What skills do you use regularly? What do people say you do well? Everyone is the go-to person for something—what is it for you?

Go to Chapter 3 in *The WOYS? Workbook*

Your Activism Skills

Activist Randy Schutt created the *Activist Skills and Experiences Questionnaire,* a comprehensive assessment tool to allow activists to inventory their skills and experiences. Activism organizations use this assessment to find what a volunteer has done in the past and get them started using their skills in the work.

The questionnaire is in *The WOYS? Workbook,* or at http://www.vernalproject.org/papers/change/ActQuest.pdf. For this chapter, complete the section "Skills and Experiences," which is pages 1–5. Save the other parts for later.

Go to Chapter 3 in *The WOYS? Workbook*

You may discover you have performed many of these tasks already. Or you may feel woefully unprepared for this work. Don't worry. You are not a professional activist, trained to make a change in the world and although you may wonder whether you have activism skills, you do. You will find your place to make a difference.

Skills You Can Apply to Activism

Now that you've completed the *Activist Skills and Experiences Questionnaire* section go back to the beginning and ask yourself if you have performed these skills in life areas unrelated to activism. For example, look at these items from the questionnaire and how you can develop the same skills outside of activism.

~ If you can cook Thanksgiving dinner for your extended family, then you can plan a community meeting

~ If you can organize a group to stop a change of zoning in your town, then you can organize a boycott

~ If you can go door to door to ask neighbors to donate to the March of Dimes, then you can canvass for a political candidate

~ If you can teach someone how to run a copy machine, then you can teach someone how to keep membership records

Don't discount the skills you have already, even if you developed them in situations unlike activism. What do people say you do well? What are you the go-to person for? Add a dash of knowledge specific to your cause, and you are ready. Shrug off those doubts and use your skills to make a change.

Go to Chapter 3 in *The WOYS? Workbook*

Your Skill Levels

As you grew from a baby to a child to a teen and to an adult, you developed and refined your skills. For example, as a baby, you knew how to grasp but not really control the movement of the object in your hand. As a child, you learned how to use your hand to grip a pencil and form letters. As an adult, you may have further developed the control of your hands to create calligraphy or art. You increased your skill level gradually.

As you examine your skills for activism, also check the level of your ability. If you are decent at balancing your checkbook, you can manage the checkbook of your local advocacy group. But dealing with taxes or preparing financial reports needs a higher skill level. To help your cause with taxes or financial reports you must learn those skills by making this an area of personal development.

Skill Hierarchies

Some activism skills are complex, and you must learn basic skills first; using complex skills effectively is dependent on learning those basic skills. For example, I teach my kids to use the vehicle's brakes (a basic skill) before I ask them to drive on the freeway (a more complex skill).

In activism, a vital skill is educating others. To inform others about my cause, I must speak clearly, know when to give feedback and what to provide and to answer questions.

At a higher skill level, such as in structured training situations, I must organize the session, prepare written materials, present information, create videos, draw illustrations, and ease discussions.

At a high level, such as where I am trying to educate those who are not interested in my cause or are actively against my cause, I need to listen to alternate viewpoints, find areas of common concern and get the person to weigh my perspective. Many basic skills are required for this complex skill.

In summary, I may not have the skills yet to educate someone who opposes my cause in a way to gain their commitment, but I might have the skills to teach someone who hasn't formed an opinion. Over time, I can work on developing the skills necessary to move up the hierarchy.

Top-Level Activism Skills: Influence and Strategic Vision

Two top-level activism skills are influencing others and strategic vision. I call them top-level because if I put all activism skills in a hierarchy, with basic skills at the bottom and gradually more complex skills moving upward, these skills are at the top. I need basic skills to perform the top-level skills well.

Influence

The first top-level skill is the ability to influence others. Influencing others is an ultimate activism skills test, and most other activism skills are secondary to this one. For example, influencing your brother over dinner to vote for a candidate is easy if he has no preconceived notions about the candidate and trusts your opinion. In this case, the skill you need is clear oral communication.

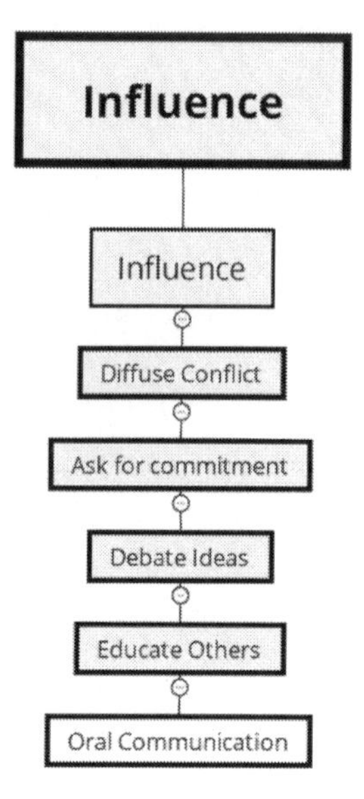

But sometimes influencing others is more difficult. Imagine trying to influence your brother to vote for your candidate if he has preconceived notions about the candidate, even if he trusts your opinion. The skills you need go beyond oral communication to educating him and effectively arguing your points.

Now imagine a situation where you are influencing a stranger to vote for your candidate. Again, this is easy if the person has no opinion and you are informed and knowledgeable. It gets tricky when they have already formed opinions, and painful when they have negative views about the candidate or about you. You need skills to diffuse conflict and ask for a commitment.

If you can influence others, you have a terrific opportunity to affect your cause, at whatever level of your skill. If you are not yet at the level of dealing with a hostile person face-to-face, and most people aren't, look at how you can use influence.

Strategic Vision

The second top-level skill is strategic vision, which is the ability to define goals and the steps needed to get there. Strategic vision is the main reason for success in social change movements and activism. The great reforms of our time, including emancipation, voting rights, and civil rights used strategic vision.[19] Successful organizers keep everyone focused on the strategic goals.[20]

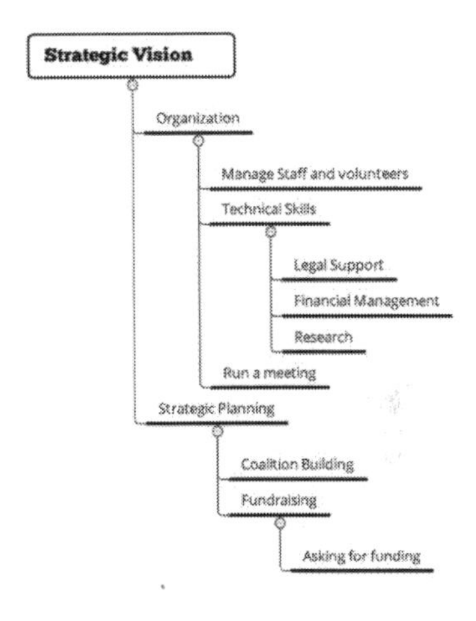

Like influencing others, the ability to create a strategic vision needs many basic skills, from running a meeting to managing staff and volunteers.

Understanding your skill level in influencing others and strategic vision helps you be more effective. For example, I know this about myself: I am not ready to influence those who are hostile to my views. Knowing about my skills allows me to choose opportunities that match my skills. I am not skilled at visioning an activism movement, but I can lay out the tasks necessary to achieve a lesser goal.

Yolanda's Story

Yolanda braids hair. Her talent is well-known in her family and community, and the intricate beauty of her designs keeps her busy with family and friends. Working as a cashier at a store is soul-sucking, so she decides to pursue hair braiding as a career. What she discovers dismays her.

Her state requires a license to braid hair. She must have a cosmetology certificate (a one-year curriculum) and pay $400 per year in professional privilege taxes.

Yolanda is already skilled at hair braiding, but she checks the curriculum and licensing requirements to see if she is missing anything. Almost all the cosmetology curriculum is unrelated to hair braiding. The licensing exam focuses in large part on handling chemicals, but Yolanda does not use chemicals on her customers' hair. So why do hair braiders need a license?

Yolanda discovers the significant advocates for hair braiding licensing are licensed cosmetologists. They have a vested interested in keeping competitors like Yolanda out of the profession, so their income stays high.

Yolanda finds an organization fighting against unnecessary occupational licensing, so more workers can earn money. When skilled workers can do work without ridiculous hurdles income inequality decreases.[21] They file a suit on Yolanda's behalf. Yolanda starts lobbying for hair braiders.

Talia's Story

Talia gathered her 20-year-old resumé and her current performance appraisals. Her resumé was from the time when she had first entered the workforce after high school, and her strong math skills and recommendations had gotten her a part-time job as a teller at the credit union. After six months she applied for and received a full-time teller position.

The credit union and the work inspired her to go back to school for a Credit Union Management two-year degree. Although taking classes one at a time while managing a full-time job was challenging, she remembers this time of her life fondly. She had lessons on credit risk, marketing, and finance but her favorite was on financial counseling. Talia believes the combination of a stimulating subject and an encouraging teacher is what led her to become a member service representative and now a loan officer.

Examining her skills from a work perspective, Talia knows she is skilled financially. She started as a teller at the credit union and advanced to her current job of loan officer because her supervisors noted how well she worked with members. She knows they view her as one of the employees who best handle the more demanding members. Talia reflects on why she is seen as a problem solver—she takes the time to listen carefully and summarize what she hears them say. Hearing their words echoed always seems to calm them, allowing Talia to move forward in solving their problem. The phrases she sees most in her performance appraisal are interpersonal skills, conflict resolution, attention to detail, and strong work ethic.

Looking through her paperwork reminds Talia of how far she has come and the skills and experience she has gained. Talia completes the Activist Skills and Experiences Questionnaire. She notices at once there are categories where she has experiences and skills related to activism, but in some she has no experience at all. Just completing the checklist reminds her of the experiences she enjoyed in the past.

She reminisces about the time as a student at her community college, when she organized a spontaneous boycott of a professor who often asked students to join in a Christian prayer during class, taught scripture as fact, and gave intelligent design as an alternative to evolution. The students contacted the administration to air their concerns but saw no changes in the classroom. So, they boycotted the class.

Talia remembers how energized she felt as she stood outside the school with her protest sign. One of the other students contacted the student newspaper and the local media. It worked. The administration brought in a replacement teacher who focused on the course material.

Returning to the present, Talia marks those skills and experiences she has from other settings and can apply to activism. She knows she can use her organizing and finance skills to help a different type of organization.

Talia decides to get feedback from friends in other areas of her life. She calls Irene, one of the college student voter registration campaign organizers, and asks to buy her coffee. She once saw Irene send a volunteer home because they were championing a candidate, a no-no during voter registration, so Talia knows she's a straight shooter.

Irene says she appreciates how Talia always shows up and is friendly. When Talia asks, Irene struggles to pick out Talia's go-to skill. She is also vague when Talia asks about the impact she is making on the cause. Talia senses that Irene doesn't really know the effect of the voter registration effort.

Talia reflects on this activism job and her participation in it. She is one of the pack and is glad to help, but she isn't sure this makes use of her unique skills or whether anyone is making much of a difference at all.

At this point in her self-assessment, Talia feels positive about having skills and knowing her history shows an ability to gain new skills and use them effectively. She decides to check out *What Color is Your Parachute?,*[22] which is a job-hunting book but also an excellent resource for becoming clear about your gifts. She had used an earlier version of the book to put together her resumé.

One exercise involves remembering seven stories, from any area or at any time in your life, where you felt positive about your accomplishments.

Talia's stories are about performing in a talent show, securing financial counseling for credit union members, organizing a boycott, receiving an A in a challenging class, organizing a major event at her church, creating her backyard garden, and decorating a train set for her son for Christmas.

For each story, she reflects on what she was trying to do, any problems and how she overcame them, and the eventual result. It feels fantastic to remember times in the past when she'd worked hard and felt proud of the achievements.

She lists the skills she used in each scenario. For example, when she decorated her son's train set for Christmas she initiated (came up with the idea), consulted (worked with her husband), used imagination (envisioned a snow-covered Christmas scene), and applied creativity (used a Christmas tree candle as the 'town' tree). Her son was so enchanted with the decorations he didn't notice his presents under the tree.

The skills she used the most often through the seven stories were: follow through, advise, assess, empathize, interview, organize, create, work with numbers, solve problems, and consult.

Finally, Talia looks at the top-level skills of influence and strategic vision. Starting with Influence, she feels comfortable and skilled at influencing others if they are open to it. She has less comfort with influencing others who have a different opinion or stance, although she believes she can listen and understand their point of view.

Switching to strategic vision, Talia does not have much experience with envisioning a movement and planning out how to achieve the end goal. She is excellent at organizing and working with other people.

Combining all she learned about her skills Talia prioritized them for her final skills list:

1. Listening
2. Using empathy
3. Interviewing
4. Working with numbers
5. Organizing
6. Consulting
7. Assessing needs
8. Advising clients
9. Being creative
10. Solving problems

Your Skills

Take stock of what you bring to activism. This serious look at your gifts is so you can make the best match in your activism and the most impact on your cause. You can prepare for your activism better by knowing your skills.

Many skills are required in an effective social justice movement. Adam Rothschild describes how a tiny group of "superstar" abolitionists:

> *...was responsible for the historic evil of slavery being banned not just in England but indirectly around the world, and in little more than a hundred years. But that group, he repeatedly emphasizes, was supported by the work of thousands of other activists who were doing pretty much what activists continue to do to this day: holding demonstrations, giving speeches, writing letters, doing legislative work, speaking through the press, providing financial support, selling socially-conscious products...*

> *and risking life and liberty taking direct action to help individual slaves. The vast majority of these activists are unknown to history, and yet, working alongside the superstars, they halted one of history's most monumental evils.*[23]

Reverend Dr. William Barber, in his passage at the beginning of this chapter, reminds you to "know your history, practice the moves of those who have gone before you, and make their music your own." He recognizes the need to understand what skills are essential to make change. Imagine a thriving activism event without technology support, research, planning, caregiving, and bookkeeping.

If you have coached a soccer team, you have the skills to manage a team-based activism effort. If you have pulled together the company holiday dinner and party, then you have the skills to organize a protest.

Your skills are the foundation of your impact.

Chapter Summary

One way to identify the best activism opportunities for you is to determine what skills you possess that can contribute to change. These might be skills you've used in activism or skills you've used in other areas of your life that you can apply to your activism.

Learn about skills hierarchies (skill levels), assess your current abilities, and decide where you want to grow and progress in the future.

Yolanda wanted to use her skills to support her family, but she ran into bureaucratic roadblocks. So, instead, she used her skills to make change for licensing reform. Talia found inspiration in reminding herself how she can use her skills to make a difference.

I hope you were able to list the three to five skills you can apply to activism immediately. In the next chapter, you will focus on your knowledge.

Activist in Action: Sue Klaus

Try and focus your energy on one or two main things that mean something to you. If you're actually involved in the process, you may be a little bit more effective. ~ Sue Klaus

Why did you choose your activism cause?

Unfortunately, my cause chose me. When I was diagnosed in 1983 with chronic fatigue syndrome, I knew that I had to do something.

Before that point, I had marched against nuclear power and for peace. I also built a Wikispaces page called Think Peace Choose Peace, which I now have to find a new home for, since Wikispaces is going away.

I wanted to do some support group meetings on the eastern or southern side of town, which was a little closer to me. I think I had one or two meetings with one or two people showing up. It's hard to show up for anything with this illness.

How did you decide what method to use for your activism?

The internet made it a lot easier to find other people with the same problem. I made some videos for Awareness Month when YouTube came into view. And now I can collect and distribute articles and videos from patients and doctors alike, worldwide, on Twitter and Facebook, to advance awareness.

I make a point of forwarding new research articles to select organizations like the AMA, Mayo, and Kaiser, and all the large medical institutions in Chicago because we need more research done here. DePaul's studies have been awesome, but other facilities in Chicago could certainly provide treatment as well as research.

Were there areas where you felt unprepared for your work?

Every single time, I felt out of my depth. I did it anyway. I'm pretty stubborn.

What advice do you have for new activists?

Try and focus your energy on one or two main things that mean something to you. If you're actually involved in the process, you may be a little bit more effective. Then focus on the things you know you can do or the things you know you can try. A little self-knowledge can come in handy here, maybe you enjoy making videos, or maybe you really enjoy writing instead. Go with your strengths.

Sue Klaus is a software support technician in Illinois, who also does advocacy and awareness work for fellow patients with MEcfs (Myalgic Encephalomyelitis). She was instrumental in her city library being rebuilt to serve her community better, and currently serves on her parishes' financial council. Sue has sung with choirs, acted on stage and in independent films, and has also self-published a small volume of her writings over the years. She is a songwriter and has also made many YouTube videos.

CHAPTER 4

Inventory Your Activism Knowledge

...ignorance, allied with power, is the most ferocious enemy justice can have. ~James Baldwin [24]

Objective

Inventory your activism knowledge.

Examine your cultural competence in preparation for your activism.

Goal

Inventory your activism knowledge. List three to five specialties.

Examine your cultural competence and list three to five areas for growth.

IN THE PAST TWO CHAPTERS, you have worked on focusing your passion and pinpointing your skills. In this chapter, you will determine the knowledge you bring to activism. To gather information, you may enjoy a deep dive into the topic and want to know everything. Or perhaps you are a "surfer" who loves to learn a bit about many areas. Both approaches are excellent and help guide your unique activism.

Everyone in activism needs cultural competence to make an impact. You will examine how you connect with those of diverse cultural backgrounds, recognize where you hold privilege and how it affects your work, and pinpoint your areas of growth.

Your Activism Knowledge

First, let me reassure you that you don't need activism expertise to start. When you decide your best activism match, you'll learn what you need. Self-education to prepare for your work is covered in Chapter 10. People must ensure they are educated and not, as James Baldwin says, "ferocious enemies of justice." Have a learning mindset instead.

To inventory your activism knowledge, complete the 'Activist Knowledge and Experiences" part of the questionnaire. The knowledge portion of the inventory is in *The WOYS? Workbook*. This inventory of your knowledge will:

- ~ remind you of knowledge you've gained in your life.
- ~ remind you why you gained this knowledge and whether you can translate it to activism.
- ~ prepare you to talk with others about what you know.

First, you will check your areas of knowledge. You will recall, for example, if you know about the significant social change movements in history, political systems, and what groups are working on change.

Go to Chapter 4 in *The WOYS? Workbook*

If you have a lot of knowledge or experience in an area, ask yourself if this is related to your passions. For example, perhaps you have a decent amount of knowledge about patriarchy and sexism. You wrote a high school English paper about the subject. When you are browsing on Facebook, you tend to follow links to articles on the subject. How does your interest in this topic relate to your Activism Passions from Chapter 2?

If you have little knowledge or experience in an area, mull over whether you have any passion for this cause. For example, if you mark "none" in the entire section on economics, perhaps it is not the best choice for you. Leave economics to others.

You also get information about your activism knowledge from inventorying the types of publications and blogs you read, what media you watch, what links you follow on social media, what groups you join, and what podcasts you enjoy. The information you choose to avoid is also informative. Topics you dodge are not worthy choices for your activism.

Cultural Competence

Cultural competence is essential for any activism. As you navigate the world, seek to understand others' cultural backgrounds. This is a way to ensure you connect better with others and find areas of agreement on your issue, and potentially an area on which to build influence for your cause. Cultural competence leads to better trust and responsiveness to a message.

Someone with cultural competence:

~ Knows their own cultural biases and assumptions and gauges their skills and comfort level in dealings with others
~ Learns about other cultures
~ Tries to understand others' experiences when working together and avoids hoisting their own experiences on others
~ Is willing to reflect on their biases and assumptions

You must prepare to broaden your understanding of other cultures to make your message more effective. This starts with understanding your background and culture and its impact on your attitudes and behavior.

Since I am a white activist, I must know how I have benefited from my privilege in the past and anticipate how the way I communicate and work with others may impact them or clash with their preferred styles. I must adjust my worldview. Diversity in activism succeeds, just as research shows diverse for-profit organizations flourish.

Differences in culture may impact the ways you communicate and learn. Dutch Sociologist Geert Hofstede researched how cultures differ and the impact of those differences on connections with one another.[25]

First in Hofstede's framework, in the dimension of power distance, one culture may see individuals as more equal, and other cultures may see distance between individuals. The United States has low power distance due to the general feeling of all "are created equal." Americans are more likely to challenge authority. In high power distance areas, such as Latin countries, challenging someone higher in the hierarchy is inappropriate. They are more comfortable with formal relationships between people and treating others with respect.

Hofstede's dimension of individualism versus collectivism describes how interdependent we are. Americans are individualists, focused on "what's in it for me," while in Latin American and Asian collectivist cultures, the group is valued over the individual. In individualist cultures expressing one's opinion is crucial, while in collectivist cultures people are more sensitive to communicating ideas disagreeable to others. They value group harmony.

Another dimension is related to uncertainty avoidance and describes how comfortable a culture is with new experiences. Americans are more comfortable with trying new things. The culture supports the idea of, as Nike purports, "Just do it." Japanese culture is high on uncertainty avoidance, and people are more thoughtful about making a change. These differences affect decision making about activist causes. In the United States, I am more willing to try something new to see how it works, while in Japan activists move more slowly and take a thorough look at how similar things were done in the past.

Finally, cultural differences occur in high-context vs. low-context communication; in high-context cultures such as North America and Western Europe, dialogue tends to be open, overt, and focused on straightforward messages. In low context cultures such as Asian and Middle Eastern, the connection is more reserved and implicit, with the nonverbal language being important.

Some cultural groups are more comfortable with a high degree of verbal confrontation and argument; others stress balance and harmony in relationships and shun confrontation. For some, forceful, direct communication can seem rude and disrespectful. Many Native American and Latino culture groups value cooperation and agreeableness. Members often avoid disagreement, contradiction, and disharmony within the groups. [26]

I must consider cultural differences in how I get my point across as a first step toward making a connection. Religion, self-identity, support networks, family, socio-economic status, gender roles, sources of information, and history have an impact on activism.

Privilege

Privilege is a complicated concept derived from being an identity group member. I like this definition:

Privilege is a system that gives unearned advantages, favors, and benefits to members of dominant groups at the expense of members of target groups, and it operates on personal, interpersonal, cultural, and institutional levels. In the United States, privilege is often granted to people who are members of particular identity groups, such as: White people, Able-bodied people, Heterosexuals, Males, Christians, Middle and upper-class people, Middle-aged people, and English-speaking people. [27]

Your cultural competence and privilege: Why it matters

I have privilege related to being white, able-bodied, heterosexual, middle-class, and English-speaking. As I am aware of my privilege, I can also honor the areas in which I don't hold privilege. I have the advantages of privilege in several areas and experience oppression in others. "White privilege is like an invisible weightless knapsack of special provisions, assurances, tools, maps, guides, codebooks, passports, visas, clothes, compass, emergency gear, and blank checks."[28]

I must also recognize in the areas where I hold privilege I may not pay attention to issues that do not affect me. The Daring Discussions Handbook reminds us,

Holding privilege is what allows us to avoid and ignore issues that do not directly affect us, and understanding your own privilege is an important part of giving others space to share difficult and vulnerable truths about their experience. [29]

What's On Your Sign?

One way to reflect on privilege is to recall times when you've been valued and times when you've been on the margins.

- Consider a time in your life when your presence, your skills, and your ideas mattered. How did you know you mattered? How did that feel? How did you respond?
- Consider a time in your life when you felt marginalized, on the margins, and believed that your presence, your ideas, your skills, and your opinions were not important. What were the circumstances? What gave you the impression that your contributions didn't matter? How did you feel? How did you respond?
- As you contrast the two situations, what strikes you? What was your level of engagement, energy, creativity, and imagination in each case? Are there conclusions you can draw from the two different experiences?

Recognize how understanding culture impacts you and those with whom you work.[30]

Go to Chapter 4 in *The WOYS? Workbook*

Evaluate your privilege

At the website *It's Pronounced Metrosexual,* you can find examples of situations that mean you have privilege.[31]

Gender

If you are male (and a man), listed below are benefits that result from being born with that gender and sex.

- ~ If you have a bad day or are in a bad mood, people aren't going to blame it on your sex.
- ~ You can be careless with your money and not have people blame it on your sex.
- ~ You can be a careless driver and not have people blame it on your sex.
- ~ You can be confident that your coworkers won't assume you were hired because of your sex.

Cisgender

If you identify with the gender you were assigned at birth, here are unearned benefits you get that many folks do not.

- ~ You can reasonably assume that you will not be denied services at a hospital, bank, or other institution because the staff does not believe the gender marker on your ID card to match your gender identity.
- ~ You can go to places with friends on a whim knowing there will be bathrooms there you can use.

Race

If you are white in the U.S., here are unearned benefits you get that many folks do not.

- You are favored by school authorities.
- You learn about your race in school.
- You can find children's books that overwhelmingly represent your race.

Sexual Orientation

If you're heterosexual, these are unearned benefits you get that folks with other sexualities do not.

- You get immediate access to your loved one in case of accident or emergency.
- People support you for an intimate relationship (e.g., congratulations on an engagement).
- You can express affection in most social situations and not expect hostile or violent reactions from others.

Ability

If you are able-bodied, these are unearned benefits you get that folks with disabilities or chronic conditions do not.

- You do not have to worry about your energy or pain level.
- You do not worry about the reactions of others to your needs.
- Strangers don't stare at you because you look different.
- You can move for long distances or on a variety of surfaces without inconvenience/discomfort/pain and at a pace considered "appropriate" by others.

Socio-economic status

If you are middle- to upper-class, these are unearned societal benefits you get that folks in lower economic classes do not.

~ Politicians pay attention to your class and fight for your vote in election seasons.

~ If you see something advertised that you want, you will buy it.

~ In the case of a medical emergency, you won't have to decide against visiting a doctor or the hospital due to economic reasons.

~ You don't have to worry that teachers or employers will treat you poorly or have negative expectations of you because of your class.

~ The schools you went to as a kid had updated textbooks, computers, and a solid faculty.

Religion

If you're a Christian in the US, these are unearned benefits you get that members of other faiths (or non-religious people) do not.

~ You can expect to have time off work to celebrate religious holidays.

~ Music and television programs about your religion's holidays are readily accessible.

~ It is easy to find stores that carry items that enable you to practice your faith and celebrate religious holidays.

~ You aren't pressured to celebrate holidays from another faith that may conflict with your religious values.

Go to Chapter 4 in *The WOYS? Workbook*

Steps for dismantling privilege

I spent years being an ostrich with my head in the sand about my privilege. When my children were born, I became oversensitive to lousy news and indications of social injustice and reacted by tuning out the story and focusing on my busy life as a full-time employee, spouse, and mother to two children. It took the 2016 election to shock me out of my comfort zone and make me realize that I make the change I want. My privilege protected me for a long time.

Dismantling privilege will not happen overnight. But here are steps for how you can start to make a difference:

- Name it! Grapple with understanding what privilege is for you and how it works in your everyday life.
- Deal with it! When you identify privilege, address it, and take some personal responsibility for not allowing it to continue.

Reframe it! Build new roles, practices, shared values, and relationships with others to counteract privilege.[32]

Go to Chapter 4 in *The WOYS? Workbook*

Cultural Competence and Privilege in Activism

Be open to broadening your worldview. The first step is to understand your background. Be aware of where you hold privilege and where you experience oppression.

Privilege provides you with advantages but can be a disadvantage to activism. Activist Rex Burkholder writes,

> *"My allies helped me realize that I was unconsciously trying to use the same strategies to get my way — using my whiteness and education as a means of power. When I was working in low-income and minority communities, this blew up in my face. Entitlement shows to others, even if you can't see it."* [33]

Recognize how culture affects you and those with whom you work. Reflect on power distance, individuals vs. collectivist focus, uncertainty, and context styles when you communicate with those from other cultural backgrounds.

Cultural competence means being aware of cultural differences in all your interactions. Cook recommends the use of the mnemonic RESPECT to remember how to interact with others in a culturally aware manner (adapted here):[34]

Respect	Understand how respect is shown within cultural groups and show that respect.
Explanatory model	Understand how people see the origins of their beliefs and reactions to injustice. How do their beliefs differ from yours?
Sociocultural context	Understand how the person's race, religion, gender, and cultural indicators impact their beliefs about injustice. How do their beliefs differ from yours?
Power	Acknowledge power differentials, if any.
Empathy	Show empathy for their point of view. You can do this without actually agreeing with their beliefs. Listen and let them be heard.

Identify Areas for Growth

Use these questions to pinpoint areas of growth in cultural competence:

- How do you work to understand your privilege and how it impacts you?
- How have you dealt with a situation in which you recognized privilege being used and tried to stop it?
- How can you work to build practices that counteract privilege?

List three to five areas for growth.

Go to Chapter 4 in *The WOYS? Workbook*

Kyle's Story

Kyle left the meeting feeling frustrated again. Although he believes those involved in helping improve race relations in his town are motivated and unselfish, it frustrates him when their privilege gets in the way of working for justice. For example, Kyle cringed when Bart talked in length about how he taught English as a second language during his gap year in Costa Rica. That doesn't make him an expert in oppression. Kyle gets irritated when white people talk about the injustices they witness and don't realize they'll never understand the life of a black person. He wishes they would recognize their privilege and how it affects their worldview. They would be much better activists.

Talia's Story

Talia completed the Knowledge and Experience part of the questionnaire. She does not have much knowledge backed up by social change experience. She has knowledge of cooperative ownership because of her work in the credit union, but she has not been involved in social change in this area.

Undaunted by her lack of knowledge, Talia believes she can learn the specifics of whatever issue she chooses.

Cultural Competence and Privilege

Talia takes the BuzzFeed quiz *How Privileged Are You?*[35] and gets this result:

> *You're quite privileged. You've had a few struggles, but overall your life has been far easier than most. This is not a bad thing, nor is it something to be ashamed of. But you should be aware of your advantages and work to help others who don't have them. Thank you for checking your privilege.*

While the result was not surprising to Talia, the questions on this quiz were eye-opening. She knows she has privilege for her race, but she was less aware of other areas of potential privilege and what those without privilege experience. These items made her stop and think:

- I have never been the only person of my race in a room.
- I have never pretended to be "just friends" with my significant other.
- I make more money than my professional counterparts of a different gender.
- I have never been homeless.
- I've never skipped a meal to save money.
- I do not have any physical disabilities.
- I do not have any learning disabilities.
- I have never taken medication for my mental health.
- There is a place of worship for my religion in my town.
- I have never been cyber-bullied for any of my identities.

Talia inventories her privilege as white, American, heterosexual, Christian, middle-class, and able-bodied. She finds herself moved by the idea that she enters the world with this privilege without doing anything. Her oldest son is dyslexic, and she knows how much it interferes with his daily life.

Talia takes the *Anti-Defamation League Personal Self-Assessment of Anti-Bias Behavior*[36] and names several areas where she can grow. She believes she has not made the time to educate herself about the culture and experiences of other groups. She recalls how people of Hispanic heritage are joining the credit union and how understanding their cultural background would have helped her serve them better.

Her areas of growth include:

~ self-education about other cultures, starting with the Hispanic population in her area
~ growing comfortable discussing racism
~ noticing bias in the media and in her environment
~ reminding herself to use inclusive language

Chapter Summary

Knowledge of your activism cause is essential to being effective. You identified your passions and skills in the previous two chapters, and in chapter 4 you determine the knowledge you bring to activism. While you can add knowledge through self-education or training courses, your inventory of current knowledge, even if it is minimal, will help make decisions about your activism path.

In addition to knowledge related to your cause, you must understand how to navigate through cultural differences while making change.

Assess your level of cultural competence and privilege. Successful activists are culturally competent. Cultural competence is essential for new activists who have several areas of privilege in their lives. You learn how to broaden your worldview, inventory your privilege, and understand how to work with people from diverse backgrounds.

Kyle's frustration shows you the importance of making sure you understand your privilege and biases while doing activism work. Talia's story illustrates the power of reflecting on cultural competence and privilege.

Activism knowledge and cultural competence are tools you need in your activism work. Were you able to list three to five areas of knowledge that you might apply to activism? I hope you were able to assess your cultural competence and list three to five areas of growth.

In the next chapter, you will explore your personal motivations so you can get the most out of your activism.

Activist in Action: Nathan Higdon

Activism work, once you commit yourself, is a lifelong endeavor. You will get tired, you will fall down, but you must get back up. That means grounding yourself, finding champions to keep you going, and realizing that many individuals do not get the white, male privilege of being able to step away from the struggle. ~ Nathan Higdon

Why did you choose your activism cause?

I grew up in East Tennessee, and it has always been more conservative than my personal values and belief system. Social justice, community activism, and progressive politics tend to run together, such that activists see one another over and over until the causes in small towns build capacity together. I think community activism, as a whole, found me.

How did you decide what method to use for your activism?

I have run for office, and I realized that my favorite part of politics is actually behind the scenes. I am a serial entrepreneur, and a political campaign is just like a lean startup business. A well-run campaign is just a well-orchestrated marketing campaign. I am simply attempting to sell a product that people need, but don't necessarily want to have to deal with buying. Unlike a roll of toilet paper, the product talks, which makes a marketing conversion more difficult.

Were there areas where you felt unprepared for your work?

In all of the work I do, I have felt most unprepared when I have gone into a situation with the intent to bring my change, instead of asking what others want, and if they, in fact, want change.

What advice do you have for new activists?

I initially dealt with "white guilt" and wanting to be a "white savior," until I learned to get past that to become effective. You must ground yourself in restorative practice. It can be exercise, yoga, meditation, or whatever helps you relax. Activism work, once you commit yourself, is a lifelong endeavor. You will get tired, you will fall down, but you must get back up. That means grounding yourself, finding champions to keep you going, and realizing that many individuals do not get the white, male privilege of being able to step away from the struggle. If you can come to realize and appreciate that the work you do is not yours, but it was likely started and lived long before you and will be here long after you, then you can prepare yourself for the long, slow process of effecting change.

Nathan Higdon received his Ph.D. in Business Administration from Oklahoma State University. He is Chairman and CFO at L'Espace, Inc. In addition to being active in politics, he is a director of the Tennessee Equality Council, Governor of the Appalachian District of Civitan International and vice chair of the Blount County Democratic Party.

CHAPTER 5

Be Clear About Your Motivation for Activism

Being in service and being involved in something that is greater than you is what makes a person complete and whole. ~Rita Moreno, actor, singer, dancer [37]

Objective

Perform a self-assessment of your motivation for activism.

Goal

List three to five motivators for your activism.

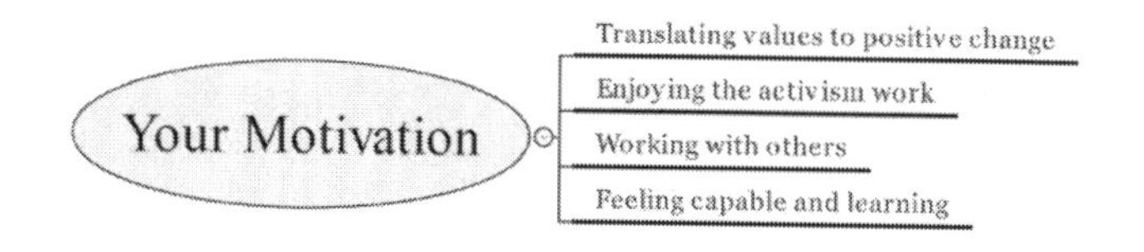

IN THE LAST SEVERAL CHAPTERS you have worked on pinpointing the gifts you bring to activism—passion, skills, experiences, and knowledge. Here you will explore personal motivation; the "what's in it for me" aspect of your work. I will review the typical activist motivation to better enable you to match your motives to those who are making change successfully. And in hopes your ultimate activism work makes a significant impact, I will review the research results related to motivation in activism.

Motivation for Activism

What's in it for me?

This sounds selfish for someone interested in activism, doesn't it? But it's not. Research shows long-term volunteers focus on the things they receive from their efforts.[38]

As the Gamaliel staff taught me, activism is difficult and unrewarding at times, but your passion for your cause will get you through the tough times.

Self-motivation matters. Your needs fuel your passion. Experiencing those needs and fulfilling them is perfectly fine. Your values, motivations, and emotions trigger the obligation to contribute and help others.[39]

Personal motivations for activism include:

~ Translating values into positive change
~ Getting satisfaction from the activism work itself
~ Enjoying working with others
~ Feeling capable and learning [40]

Translating values into positive change.

In Chapter 2 you identified your values and passions for making change. The opportunity to translate those values and passions into activism work will motivate you. Activists often value helping those who don't have the same privilege. Other activists focus on different issues, such as on a passion for young girls to grow up believing they are as worthy as young boys.

If you have a passion for your cause, you can describe strong feelings and emotions about it. Remember the discussion about what breaks your heart? You use these feelings and emotions as motivators in doing activism. Your idealism takes you into the right activist role.

Getting satisfaction from the activism work itself

Feeling satisfaction from work itself is a powerful motivator. It is lovely to be needed. Sometimes the activism work is exciting. And sometimes escaping your life and working for others feels right.

People motivated by the work itself are likely to work hard and push themselves to support a cause. Motivation from inside rather than from an outside source, such as a paycheck, is stronger and lasts longer.

Perhaps your satisfaction comes from mattering, the idea that you are the person you were meant to be; that you are fulfilling your potential. The right opportunity makes you feel you are essential in the world and were born for a reason.

Enjoying working with others

We have a built-in need to socialize.[41] Activism and volunteering with friends or family can be motivating, even if you are working on their cause rather than yours.

Serving others builds a rewarding connection between people, even without the bonus of making a change in the world. This type of sociability is a blessing to yourself and others; it can make even the most laborious tasks feel sacred.

It can even improve your mental and physical health. Helping others may contribute to better physical and psychological health through the connections made with one another. [42] Strong social networks can improve health, reduce stress, and improve self-esteem.[43]

Feeling capable and learning

Feeling capable motivates you. You focused on your skills in Chapter 2, but here you will examine the idea that knowing you are capable is part of your motivation for a task. And if you achieve your goals for activism, you will experience increased self-esteem. The skills you bring to activism, when used to make change, will motivate you to continue to do more.

Learning new skills along the way may motivate you. The skills you learn may help you in other areas of your life, too.

Getting out in the world and making change happen is "what makes a person whole," according to award-winning actor, singer, and dancer Rita Moreno. It is challenging and perhaps is an essential need of yours. Although challenging yourself is uncomfortable, at day's end, you can reflect on what you learned from stepping out of your comfort zone.

The WOYS? Workbook contains a professional survey entitled *Bales Volunteerism-Activism Scale*. Completing this will give you more feedback on what activism factors motivate you.

Go to Chapter 5 in *The WOYS? Workbook*

Carol's Story

After the election, those opposed to Trump's administration resisted in a variety of ways. Although Carol lives in a deep red state, she still believes in the power of democracy and the necessity to make her voice heard by her elected representatives. Carol organized a postcard-writing group who meet every week at a local coffee house. Another organizer scours the news each week and prepares an action list for postcard writers to use. The organizers provide postcards, pre-addressed mailing labels, stamps, and a volunteer to haul the postcard stack to the post office. The group averages about 75 postcards mailed each week.

Translating values into positive change

It is hard to tell how much impact 1 or 75 postcards will make on pressing issues such as health care and immigration. Although Carol's lovingly crafted postcard missives may have touched the heartstrings of elected representatives, she doesn't know how many reacted. She knows many chose not to vote the way she suggested. However, she does know from research what representatives say affects their views on issues. A 2011 study by the Congressional Management Foundation shows in-person visits from constituents are the most effective approach to influencing their opinions. But since she cannot visit all her elected representatives and she doesn't like to talk on the phone, she goes with postcards, which are lower on the Congressional Management Foundation list of useful methods.

Satisfaction from the activism work itself

She works on advertising the postcard-writing opportunity, bringing supplies, and greets each volunteer. This activism type fits for her because she likes working with other people (she also enjoys the coffee house's chai tea lattes).

Enjoyment from working with others

Although the goal is serious, the work is fun and social. It is a pleasant way to do activism. Even her teenage children come occasionally, and she enjoys sharing the experience with them.

Feeling capable and learning

Carol believes she is learning a great deal about the issues from reading each week's action list. She also appreciates the lively conversations and debates during the session. Candidates sometimes show up to write postcards and talk about their positions. And she is becoming skilled at writing a concise statement of her stance on many issues.

Risk-Taking

Your comfort with risk-taking may inform the activism choices you make. You must appreciate the risks of your cause.

I'm sure I won't use violence or put my safety or others at risk. That may change as I progress in my activism, but I know my starting point. But perhaps I can nudge myself into a little more risk than I am comfortable with in support of my cause: add a bumper sticker to my car, challenge a person's views face-to-face, and ask others directly to support my cause.

Some activism is low-risk, such as sharing an article on Facebook a few of your Friends see as negative. And then arguing with Friends of Friends about it.

Other activism is high-risk, such as Rosa Park's refusal to give up her seat on the bus.[44] Potentially risky, protests about police misconduct or the need for gun control are necessary nonetheless.[45]

Journalists and human rights protestors experience danger in particular regions of the world. And certain people, such as the LGBTQIA+ community, women, and indigenous people are targeted with violence simply because of their cultural identity. [46]

Go to Chapter 5 in *The WOYS? Workbook*

Support Network

You will create a support network to help you in your activism work. This is a networking opportunity, a way to get feedback on your skills, what you are trying to do, and improving the odds of finding the right match for you.

If you are a social person, you already have a network of contacts from which to tap team members. Consider also those you've worked with who know your day-to-day skills and how you work with others. Don't pick those who only know your pleasing side. Friends who know your good points (you did a fantastic job planning the holiday party) and bad points (yelling makes you angry) are valuable resources.

Social media is an excellent way to get support and information. LinkedIn is a place to find others who can help. Share a Facebook post with friends who can help you make connections.

Include your best friends, just for moral support. Who is an ally in your life? Who supports you and is honest and loving? Who gives you a little push when you doubt yourself? These friends are the most valuable support group members.

As Pat Summitt, long-time head coach of the University of Tennessee's Lady Vols basketball team said,

> *The absolute heart of loyalty is to value those people who tell you the truth, not just those people who tell you what you want to hear. In fact, you should value them most. Because they have paid you the compliment of leveling with you and assuming you can handle it.*[47]

Go to Chapter 5 in *The WOYS? Workbook*

Talia's Story

Personal Motivation

Talia reviewed the four areas of personal motivation and ranked them. For her, translating her values into positive change has been missing from her activism.

1. Translating values into positive change
2. Enjoying working with others
3. Feeling capable and learning
4. Getting satisfaction from the activism work itself

Motivation for Activism

Bales Volunteer-Activism Scale

Talia's results: Her score was highest for Idealism/Philosophical Commitment and lowest for Sense of Effectiveness. This corresponds to the way she ranked translating values into positive change. She was surprised to see Sense of Effectiveness as her lowest motivator, as she had rated satisfaction from the work itself highly. But in general, her personal motivation rankings match up well with her results from the *Bales Volunteer-Activism Scale.*

Risk-taking

Talia does not want to take risks, at least at this point in her life.

Support Network

Talia's Support Network includes her best friend, her husband, a professor from a financial counseling class who has been a valued mentor, and a friend from church who she has enjoyed working with on several projects. She will keep open the possibility of adding other people to her network.

Chapter Summary

It is okay to satisfy your personal needs when doing activism. In fact, it may be the way that you can establish a role in change that suits you and keeps you engaged long term. You should know what needs are important to you to stay motivated and productive. Research supports linking personal motivation with activism motivation. Because activism can be challenging, personal motivation helps you get through the tough times.

Identify your motivation in the areas of translating values into positive change, enjoying working with others, feeling capable and learning, and gaining satisfaction from activism work.

Carol used her motivation to start an advocacy/social group at her local coffee house. Talia performed her motivation self-assessment and realized her final activism choice must stay rooted in her values.

In the next chapter, you will craft your ideal activism opportunity.

PART 3

Your Activism Options

In Part 3 you imagine your ideal activism and start the search for the right opportunity to match your gifts.

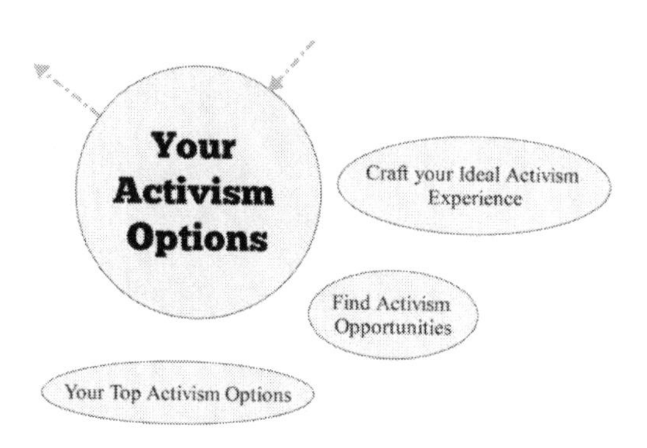

Part 3 includes:

Chapter 6: Craft Your Ideal Activism Opportunity

Chapter 7: Find Activism Opportunities

Chapter 8: Narrow Your Activism Opportunities

CHAPTER 6

Craft Your Ideal Activism Opportunity

Change will not come if we wait for some other person or some other time. We are the ones we've been waiting for. We are the change we seek. ~Barack Obama [48]

Objective

Create a vision of your ideal activism opportunity.

Goal

List the characteristics of your ideal activism opportunity.

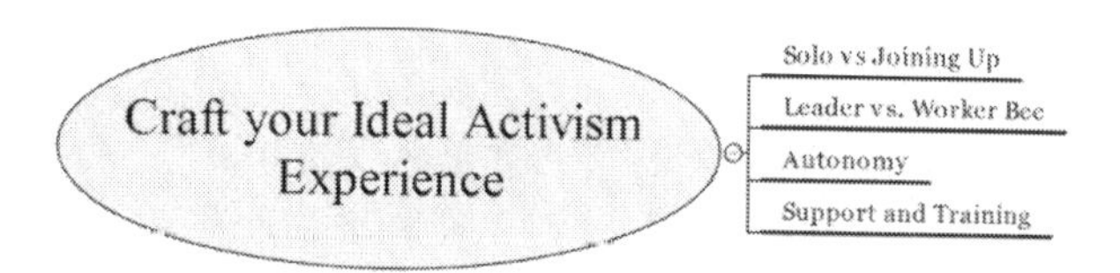

IN THIS CHAPTER, YOU WILL DECIDE what type of activism experience suits you. Do you want to create your own opportunity, or would you instead work with others in an established movement? What does a perfect day in activism look like to you?

The best option for you

You have many choices about where to start with your activism, but the right place for you is the one best matched to your passion, skills, knowledge, and motivation. Stay true to the work you've done so far to understand what drives you and what you bring to activism. With focus, you can evaluate what is right for you and, in turn, maximize the impact you can make. You are unique, different from every other human on Earth, and your uniqueness is your superpower.

Focus on your passions is essential because of the magnitude of needs bombarding you. It comes from family and friends asking for help in their activism work. It comes from the media you consume, your social media feed, and the blogs you read. It also comes from your brain and the messages you tell yourself about making the world a better place.

Now is the time to get focused on your unique contribution to change. As President Obama said, "We are the ones we've been waiting for." Focused activism is more satisfying than reeling around responding to requests; you have better control over your time, and it makes you more effective. As activist and author Hillary Rettig states,

> *"Working on too many movements or on too many types of projects means that you will probably have to manage unwieldy amounts of information and people. By focusing, you'll gain in-depth experience in whatever type of activism you are doing—expertise that will help make you an even more effective activist."*[49]

Committing to one cause allows you to develop depth you cannot accomplish by volunteering scatter-shot.

You will pinpoint the activism cause most important to you and find the right place for your unique skills. Then you can relax, knowing you are doing your best for an issue you care about. And if your friends ask for help, or you see a protest appeal on Facebook, or your brain tells you to do more, say no if you want, because you are doing enough.

Getting what you need

You may be the next Cesar Chavez and start a successful movement. Don't discount that possibility. Dream big. That may not be your cup of tea, though. Or your unique circumstances limit the amount of time or energy you can devote to a cause. There are ways you can make an existing movement successful.

Going Solo versus Joining Up

Going Solo

One way to make an impact on the world is to create your own activism, rather than joining an existing movement. You don't need to start a large movement; instead, make a focused effort for your cause. For example, Lynne Iser created a website called Elder Activists: Creating a Thriving and Just Future. To inspire elders, she shares stories about others who are making a difference in their senior years. Along with educational resources, she lists opportunities to act in social causes.[50]

There are advantages to going solo:

- ~ You can focus on your unique issue or on your unique approach to an existing problem
- ~ It offers autonomy to use your own process and timeframe
- ~ It caters to people who like to work by themselves

- It caters to people who enjoy strategic vision and making their own way in the world

At the same time, going solo may not be the right approach:

- There is no one else to share work with and so potentially more pressure and stress
- There may be work/life balance challenges
- You get no support from an existing movement

What would tell you going solo is right for you? When you thought about your callings, did you have a clear one, with a vision? If you experienced a calling with the associated feelings of meaningfulness and fear, explore it. Don't let your calling get lost.

If you have a vision and the motivation to go solo, research the following:

- What do you need to do to get ready? Recognize the match between your skills, knowledge, and motivation and what is necessary for your vision.
- Do you need to do any training?
- What about improving your understanding in this area?
- Do you need to hire resources where you don't have an ability?

Once you decide you are ready to go solo, take this extra step. You may have all the resources in place and high motivation but make sure you are not duplicating the efforts of people who are already doing this work in the field. The chances are they have had boots on the ground longer than you. Learn from them and add your unique spin to what they are doing. It is also critical your efforts don't hinder or dilute the efforts of others.

Look at whether you need support from others already working in your cause.

> *"Being in regular relationship with local organizers and communities not only allows us to engage in accountably crafted forms of witness, advocacy, and resistance, it also can take away the energy-draining edge that the shock of learning about these oppressions can bring."*[51]

Networking with coalitions will enhance the odds of making change.

An exception to the idea of avoiding duplication of effort is when you borrow an effective activism strategy for application in your unique setting. Go ahead and adopt an effective approach and apply it in your community. Don't reinvent the wheel.

Joining up with an existing movement

Perhaps joining a current movement is the best idea for you. This works if you have limited time to devote to your cause, or if you want the social aspects of working in a team, or if a group and its efforts really light your fire.

There are advantages to joining others:

~ It adds your skills to a diverse team to make an effective organization
~ You will receive help and ideas from others
~ It offers potentially less pressure and stress because of shared work and emotional support

At the same time, joining up may not be the right approach:

- ~ There is the potential for less autonomy and the ability to work your way
- ~ The organization may not have the same ideals as you, and so the activism effort may not make the impact you wish

One way to help you decide which approach is right for you is to consider your personal motivation for activism. Check the chart below to see how your personal activism might play out in going solo and joining up.

Personal Motivation for Activism	***Going Solo***	***Joining Up***
Translating values into positive change	You have more control over whether your values are translated into personal change.	You have potentially less control over the work you do but more resources to make positive change.
Satisfaction from the activism work itself	You have control over your work and decide how you want to do it to maximize your satisfaction.	You have less control over your work and ensuring you are satisfied with it.
Enjoyment from working with others	Gaining the community you want around you will take more effort.	The community is more likely to be available to you.
Feeling capable and learning	Doing it yourself is a way to dive in and learn, but you must get the training and tools you need. Also, you must seek feedback to grow and learn.	An existing movement should give you the training and tools you need. They also should help you reflect on how you can grow as an activist.

Go to Chapter 6 in *The WOYS? Workbook*

Bill's Story

Bill is an unexpected activist ready to start combatting the reclassification of public lands to private to exploit natural resources. His motivation for activism is to make a direct impact on public policy, and his top motivator is translating values into positive change. He decides joining up is the best possibility for him because he needs the resources and support of an advocacy organization to impact this cause. Starting his own organization does not make sense since there are existing ones already working. He contacts one of them and shares his skills and knowledge so they can place him in the right work.

Ideal Activism Experiences

In the next section, you will describe your perfect activism experience. Before you do, consider what research tells us you can gain from your experience. The activist choosing to go solo can design their own activism experiences. On the other hand, if you join an existing movement, they can provide you with support.

When volunteers are recruited or show up to help a movement, what happens? How do organizations put you in the right place to match your skills, knowledge, and motivation?

Hahrie Han wrote *How Organizations Develop Activists: Civic Associations and Leadership in the 21st Century* based on her research on activist development, focusing on how organizations make an impact by better engaging activists in the work.[52]

Han's book is a resource for understanding what support you can get from organizations. She examined two different approaches to attracting activists—mobilization and organization. Mobilization is getting bodies to the right places in the activism work but not necessarily focusing on developing the skills of people.

Mobilization is essential, but the second approach, organization, in which they work to match individuals to tasks in a way to engage them, is vital to you. She believes movements adopting the organization approach to activist development are more efficient. From a big picture perspective, this approach supports democracy by investing in activism skills for everyone.

Research supports Han—successful organizations realize the impact of dedicated and talented people; they ensure activists are engaged at the highest level of skill they possess and for which they feel the most motivation. Furthermore, they continue to nurture activists to even higher levels of skills and engagement.[53]

What Han calls "high-engagement chapters" did both mobilizing and organizing, as described here:

> *First, organizers make requests for action that bring people into contact with each other and give them space to exercise their strategic autonomy... Second, and relatedly, organizers focus on building relationships and community through interdependent (as opposed to individual)*

action...Finally, because organizers want to develop people's ability to take responsibility, they focus on extensive training, coaching, and reflection, while mobilizers do not...Mobilizing and organizing are mutually reinforcing approaches. Mobilizing helps develop a prospect pool or "leads list" that can be used to find potential leaders. Organizing can enable the work of mobilizing by developing high-quality leaders capable of recruiting future activists.[54]

Activism organizations must support their activists. There are mundane tasks like making copies. There's the need to learn the ways the group wants the task done. There is the emotional support for facing daunting challenges or re-energizing after working in the cause.

In employee selection, successful companies use a research-supported method called the realistic job preview. Rather than enticing potential hires with an overly optimistic job preview, a realistic job preview gives the good and bad points, so when a candidate chooses to pursue the job, they are making an informed decision. This leads to less turnover. It also improves job satisfaction because of realistic expectations and matching job requirements with the person's skills, knowledge, and abilities.[55]

To find the right activism match, get the good points and the bad points about the opportunity, or what is called a realistic job preview for the activism. Organizations may use the wrong approach in signing up activists, a sign they don't have their act together. An organization forthright about the job might say, "90% of the work is mundane, 10% is inspiring, but we get results" rather than, "we do great activism and it's always fun." You are willing to devote your time and safety to a cause, so ferret out the organization's real story as you navigate your possibilities.

Your compatibility with a specific job and your match with their mission mean satisfaction. You are less likely to quit.[56] During your interactions with an organization see if you are a fitting match for the work and their mission.

Leaders play an essential role in creating a positive environment by developing programs to meet volunteer needs. They focus on the volunteer's values and other needs they may express.[57] Volunteers stay longer and recruit others to join the organization.[58]

In your search for an activism match, look for the benefits listed below. Organizations with these benefits are more effective and impactful. For you to make your best impact, get involved in the high-engagement type of organizations Han describes as offering these criteria:

- They will discuss the good and bad points of the opportunity
- They will strive to build a relationship with you
- They care about how you see yourself as an activist and ask you about your goals as a volunteer
- They try to help you reinforce your goals and meet your needs
- They try to bring you into contact with others, so you have a community around you
- They provide you with well-designed orientation and training to give you the information you need
- They provide the tools you need

- They provide you with work that fulfills your needs and motivates you
- They coach you as you do the work
- They give you some control over your work
- They engage you in reflection about the work

Go to Chapter 6 in *The WOYS? Workbook*

Talia's Story

Talia believes joining up rather than going solo will make more impact. This is because she has limited time due to her full-time job. But the opportunity to have more resources and community is appealing. She wants to learn more and develop as an activist, so having structure in place will work well for her.

The idea of joining a high-engagement organization like the one Han described intrigues Talia; she believes they can help her make an impact. She wishes for training on important skills and knowledge, as well as coaching and reflection along the way.

Talia knows her work schedule and other time constraints mean she may not get the ideal activism experience she wants. But because this is the "dreaming part" she pretends she doesn't have limitations.

Talia's ideal day is to work with others as a team, sharing ideas and getting feedback. But she also likes responsibility for a piece of the work she can do on her own. This will help her learn and improve her skills. At the credit union, she has access to webinars when she needs to learn, and she can take the training when she needs the information. She'd like that for her activism work, too.

Since she identified specific skills as those she is ready to use immediately, she would like to work in organizing, interviewing, or creating. But she would like to eventually learn different skills to make her more flexible. She knows learning is necessary.

She recognizes she is not a risk-taker regarding boots-on-the-ground activism, but she wants to build her confidence and skills in that area.

Although she doesn't mind a bit of drudge work, she hopes most of her activism work is the kind where she sees and experiences the change she wants to make.

Talia feels confident about asking questions and finding the right match.

Craft Your Ideal Activism Opportunity

The ideal activism experience for you will describe the characteristics of the work, such as how you work with people, what you want to learn, and your preference for level of responsibility.

Characteristics of the Activism Work

Mull over this list and craft your ideal activism opportunity:

- ~ Level of responsibility
- ~ Way in which I work with people
- ~ Ways in which I make an impact
- ~ What I want to do
- ~ What I want to learn
- ~ What support and resources I want from the organization:[59]
    - o They strive to build a relationship with me
    - o They care about how I see myself as an activist and try to help me reinforce it
    - o They try to bring me into contact with others, so I have a community around me
    - o They provide me with training
    - o They coach me as I do the work
    - o They give me some control over my work
    - o They engage me in reflection about the work and my part in it

Your Ideal Activism Experience

Pull it all together. Dream big! This is your ideal activism experience. Imagine yourself out there making change. Consider the reflection you've done so far:

- ~ Skills - the skills you want to use and learn (chapter 3)
- ~ Knowledge - the knowledge you want to use and learn (chapter 4)
- ~ Motivation - your strongest motivators (chapter 5)

Craft your ideal activism experience.

Go to Chapter 6 in *The WOYS? Workbook*

Chapter Summary

You've imagined your dream job; why not do the same for your ideal activism experience?

What will work best for you to make the change you want? Explore the advantages and disadvantages of going solo (starting your own activism work from scratch) and of joining up (becoming part of an existing movement).

What do you need for support? I describe the characteristics of high-engagement organizations—they are honest about their work, develop a relationship with you, help you meet your goals, provide support, training, and coaching, and help you grow.

Bill knows the cause he wants to support but uses the self-assessment to decide on joining an existing organization rather than embarking on a solo endeavor. Talia, for different reasons, also decides to join a current organization. Both are sure they need an organization which supports them.

In this chapter, you decided the type of activism experience that best suits you. Getting clear about the characteristics of the work means a better match with potential opportunities.

In the next chapter, you will learn about the array of activism methods from which you can choose.

Activist in Action: Carl Gombert

For me, the work always comes first. As it gets made, I start to discover what it might mean, how it might connect to larger causes or conversations, and so on. ~ *Carl Gombert*

Mule by Carl Gombert

I have been aware of and deeply interested in the power of images for a very long time, but I was never an overtly political artist. In fact, I have very mixed reactions—I admire much political/activist art but I also find much of it to be heavy-handed and/or overbearing. Moreover, I never really chose a topic or cause for activism. Rather, I made a series of works that interested me, and merely let them speak to a variety of issues.

A series of self-portraits depicting myself as different races, ethnicities, religions, social classes and occupations (collectively titled *The Real Me*) began as an alternative to written material. I was teaching a first-semester college seminar with the goal of helping students come to terms with the reality that their identity was shaped and influenced by a variety of factors, and likely differed considerably from that of their classmates. Rather than yet another article to read, I wanted primary visual sources that would allow them to talk about how they perceived and reacted to different visual cues such as skin color, hairstyle, costume, and religious symbols.

Somewhat surprisingly, the work resonated with audiences of all ages and seemed to be a very effective tool for initiating important conversations. Thus, I became an activist—I guess—for advancing the causes of racial justice and equality, but only in so far as I helped people start examining their own thoughts and preconceptions.

For me, the work always comes first. As it gets made, I start to discover what it might mean, how it might connect to larger causes or conversations, and so on. So, I am not sure I have any advice for new activists other than to pay attention, and to remember that what your work means isn't entirely up to you. An artist's intentions are important and are part of the whole package, but they are not the sole determinant of what it means or how it is perceived.

Carl Gombert was born in Brimfield, Ohio in 1959. He started taking painting lessons at the age of 14 with money he earned delivering newspapers. He completed a BFA in Drawing from the University of Akron and an MFA in Painting from Kent State University. He worked as a stagehand before earning a Ph.D. in Interdisciplinary Fine Arts at Texas Tech University. He has exhibited in more than 250 exhibitions across the US and abroad. His work is in numerous museum, collegiate, and corporate collections. Since 1993 he has taught painting, drawing, and art history at Maryville College in Tennessee.

CHAPTER 7

Find Activism Opportunities

Everybody can be great...because anybody can serve. You don't have to have a college degree to serve. You don't have to make your subject and verb agree to serve. You only need a heart full of grace. A soul generated by love. ~*Reverend Martin Luther King, Jr.* [60]

Objective

Review activism methods and choose those that motivate you.

Goal

List three to five activism methods that motivate you.

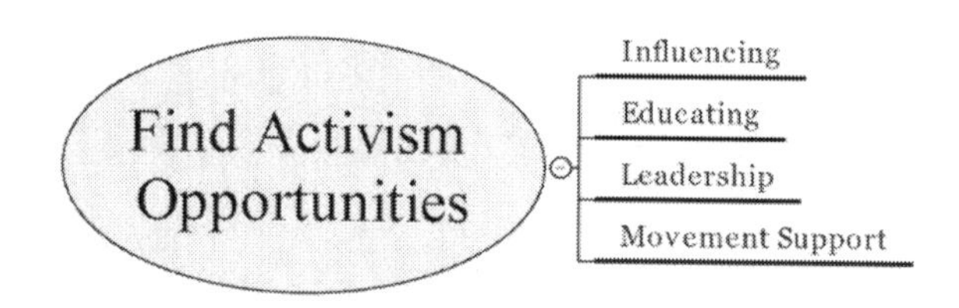

IN THIS CHAPTER, I PRESENT a variety of activism opportunities to help you decide what methods motivate you.

Activist Skills and Experiences

If you imagine opportunities for activism, you can recall iconic moments in social justice history such as Martin Luther King, Jr., and Rosa Parks in the civil rights movement. The Buddhist Monk Quang Duc, who in 1963 burned himself in the streets to protest the Vietnamese government. Anti-Slavery. Suffragists. The labor movement.

But the reality of activism is slow progress and sometimes mundane tasks such as signing up community members to vote, canvassing, or passing out flyers.

The good news is there are many opportunities for budding activists. You will make the change you wish but take the time to make the match between your passion and your best opportunity. To help you be successful with this match, learn about activism methods so you can begin to recognize what motivates you.

Influencing Others

If you are skilled at influencing others, you have a fantastic opportunity to make the change you want to see in the world.

Run for Office

People are turning out to run for office in higher numbers than ever. Stephanie Schriock is the president of Emily's List, a group helping female Democratic candidates run for office. Stephanie says the number of women who contacted her about running went from 1000 in 2016 to 22,000 since the election.[61]

Women are not equally represented in politics, even though they have an equal chance of winning if they enter. "Going into the off-year election season of 2017, women occupied just 105 of the 535 seats—19.6 percent—in the US Congress, 24 percent of statewide elective executive offices, such as governor and attorney general, and 25 percent of state legislative offices. Only 20 of the country's 100 largest cities had female mayors."[62]

"You should run." Has anyone said this to you? Perhaps consider it.

Wendy Gooditis was an unexpected politician in 2017. After hearing the incumbent speak at a town hall meeting, she expressed the opinion that someone needed to run against him. "And everybody started yelling, 'You run Wendy,'" Ms. Gooditis said, "and my husband started poking me, and then, I guess, I am in." On April 30, she had $700 in a campaign account and no staff. By Election Day she had a staff of eight and had raised almost $500,000. She defeated Mr. Minchew by about 1,000 votes out of more than 29,000 ballots cast."[63]

Lobbying

Lobbying means talking to people in government who have influence over your issues. Your goal is to state your position on the subject and persuade others to use their power on your behalf.

Tips for Effective Lobbying

1. Lobby face-to-face—According to a Congressional Management Foundation survey, elected officials are the most influenced by in-person visits from constituents; emails least affected them. [64]
2. Be prepared—Getting ready for the appointment is essential. Prepare a summary of your position.
3. Be courteous—Introduce yourself; no matter the response, be polite, because although they may not support you on this issue, they may back your cause at a later point.
4. State your purpose—Give a summary of your position, ask about their position, know what to say if they oppose, aren't sure, or support it.
5. Appeal to their moral principles—In situations where you are talking with those with different views, base your arguments on the

person's moral principles, not your own. These arguments are more persuasive.[65] If you go in strong with your ideas, the other person's stance hardens, but if you express your opinions with less certainty, the other person's position tends to soften.[66]

6. Appeal to need for affiliation—Robert Cialdini is a pioneer in persuasion research and has focused in recent years on persuasion in activism. He uses the need for affiliation to persuade homeowners to reduce their energy costs. Rather than use logic to educate them about saving resources, he tells them how their electricity usage compares to the neighbors. It works. If homeowners were using more energy than their neighbors, they lowered their usage after the comparison.

To summarize, to lobby a government official, you must show up in person, demonstrate your expertise, state your position politely and softly (to increase connection and soften their stance), and include statements about others to support the view (appeal to affiliation).

Civil Disobedience, Strikes, and Sit-ins

When I was developing an employee selection process for a church position, I ran across an interesting tip. It is common to do background checks on candidates, but this tip was to thoughtfully evaluate the less-than-spotless background reports instead of excluding them immediately. I admit I thought less-than-spotless records should mean a resounding "no." But the advice was to better understand why an applicant has a criminal record. Perhaps the candidate was arrested for civil disobedience in support of social justice. Since then I have noticed social justice activists use civil disobedience, strikes, and sit-ins as ways of gaining attention and support for their cause, and expect arrest and incarceration. For example, in July 2017, in protest of Affordable Care Act repeal, several Unitarian Universalist ministers were arrested.[67]

Civil disobedience in 2017 took the form of protesting at Standing Rock, interrupting Thanksgiving turkey pardons to protest animal rights, disrupting the Macy's Parade to oppose action against undocumented youth, and blocking a freight line in Olympia, Washington, to oppose fracking.

Sit-ins are legal forms of protest in which people take up space to bring attention to their cause; the civil rights movement started sit-ins, the most famous being in North Carolina in response to blacks being refused service at the lunch counter. Recently, the "take a knee" activism at sporting events has received energized debate. Professional athletes are influential, and they are using this type of "sit-in" as a platform for their cause.

Strikes are work stoppages used to force employers to offer better wages, benefits, and working conditions. If negotiations between a company and union break down, the union members walk off the job. This sometimes causes a work stoppage, but the company may plan to bring in replacement workers or use salaried employees to keep the operation running.

If you choose this form of activism, understand the potential consequences of the method you select. Are you prepared for arrest? Are you willing to work the picket line and forego wages to pressure management for better benefits?

Strategic Vision

Creating Your Own Activism

Strategic vision is at the top of the activist skills hierarchy and needs a sophisticated skill set. It is critical if you decide to go solo or build your own organization. Be explicit about the change you want to make and envision the end goal. From there you must remove obstacles, set goals, and create your plan. Once you implement, get feedback about impact, and make course corrections, if necessary.

Campaign Design and Management

Running a political campaign is an example of strategic vision. You must evaluate the forces supporting and opposing social change, establish specific goals, design the campaign, and evaluate its effectiveness. It is fair to say if your candidate wins, your campaign was effective, but evaluation will allow more discernment. For example, an evaluation might conclude your candidate won explicitly because of the design of your campaign.

Leadership

A lack of skilled leaders hinders activist organizations. Without enough leaders, they end up tabling work important to their movement. They need leaders who can communicate a vision, inspire performance toward a goal, recruit and develop volunteers, and make change happen.

Benjamin Todd and Roman Duda at the website 80,000 Hours say leaders impact an activism organization by letting others use their strengths for the cause.[68]

Successful leadership is not always visible to outsiders but is vital to the success of an organization. Poor leadership may show to outsiders. In the way a coffee ring on an airplane tray table makes you wonder about maintenance on the engine, a chaotic volunteer event makes you wonder about the organization's ability to make a difference for their cause.

Setting goals to achieve the mission

One way in which leaders make an impact in their organization is through setting goals to achieve the organization's mission. Getting the right parties involved in visioning outcomes helps focus the work and motivate volunteers.

Managing people

Another way leaders make an impact is through the management of people. An excellent non-profit leader can recruit able volunteers. Keeping volunteers happy and inspired to meet the organization's mission is critical as well. As discussed in Chapter 6, high-engagement organizations can meet the needs of volunteers and lengthen the time they will serve. Finally, leaders must interact with people of varying skill levels, motivations, and personalities. They must build teams, help them work together efficiently through cooperative decision making, resolve conflict, and improve processes.

Coalition Building

Another leadership skill is coalition building, which is combining efforts with groups focused on an element of the cause or a related cause. To make this happen, leaders must find practical ways for the groups to work together.

One of the skills taught at the Gamaliel workshop was how to conduct one-on-one meetings for relationship building and, ultimately, coalition. The purpose of such meetings is to better understand the other person and develop a connection by finding out their motivation, passion, ambition, fears, and obstacles.

Leaders stay open to organizations that may be an ally or a future partner in their cause. A program called SameSide organizes dinners to get activists together in a fun setting to focus on engagement instead of tasks such as fundraising. This type of environment allows connections to develop that can be useful in later activism.[69]

Leaders make an impact on their organization's success. Entire textbooks are devoted to the topic of leadership. But if you are a successful leader in other areas of life, recognize the need for excellent leaders in activism. You may make an enormous impact.

Educating Others

Educating others is a skill important in welcoming and preparing volunteers for work in activism. Teaching skills for activism work needs skill in itself. I bet you've had a situation where, instead of structured training, they told you, "you'll pick it up after a few days," or "watch

Margie." That type of instruction was probably unhelpful for learning the job.

Contrast that with training where the essential skills and the best way of learning them are identified ahead of time. In training, you get time, resources, and expert help to get you to a competent level quickly. The time and energy needed to design the training will pay off with skilled activists.

Activist Orientations

If you are an excellent teacher, support a cause by helping others get up to speed quickly. Instructional designers can help organizations name the essential skills and knowledge necessary for the activism job and create instruction that develops skills quickly. Coaching skills will help new volunteers with support as they begin the activism work.

Awareness Days

Organizations put on awareness days to focus attention on their cause. They hope providing education will result in change. Although many of these efforts are nationally focused, co-opt this approach and create an awareness day in your area.

Support Programs

Support programs rely on the motivational aspects of setting goals to support behavior change. Setting moderately difficult goals and getting feedback on your progress improves the odds of goal completion. One rule of thumb: you need 30 days of practice for a new behavior to become a habit. An example of a support program is Veganuary, which is held in the month of January and supports those trying to eat vegan.[70]

Specialized Skills

Background Research

Are you one of those folks who find the answer to a problem through research? Better yet, can you conduct research by collecting data to test a hypothesis, analyze the data, and then write an understandable report? If so, you have a tremendous opportunity to make an impact in the world of activism. Your skills can produce new research to direct social movements. Causes require a thorough program evaluation for the most impact. Any cause needs someone who can research strategic and tactical possibilities to give the best focus for everyone's efforts.

If you can add knowledge of your activism to this skill set, you will be invaluable in your cause. Certain areas of need involve complex skills or expertise, and sometimes both, to make an impact. If you have these specialized skills, pass over opportunities others can handle, and make your unique contribution.

Imagine trying to make a difference in tax lobbying and the implications for the financial capability of low-income communities. This involves a solid understanding of tax policy and economic theory. The folks at Prosperity Now do an excellent job of explaining these complex ideas and helping activists get involved in an otherwise daunting cause.[71]

Legal Intervention

Assessing legal aspects of social problems and arguing cases in court is a specialty area; one of the pillars supporting a social movement. It is a way to use skills to help others whose voices are not heard, such as the lawsuits filed in response to immigration bans. The capabilities of legal professionals can support activism in many ways, as described in this letter to law students,

> *"...the passionate advocate for victims of domestic violence, the dedicated public defender, the volunteer counsel for the victims of eviction, the legal services lawyer working with farm workers or the aging, the modestly paid counsel to the organization trying to change the laws for a living wage, or affordable housing, or the homeless or public education reforms."*[72]

News Media Outreach

Activist organizations use news media outreach as a method of giving information about the cause to a broad audience. One way to make an impact is to develop relationships with reporters who write about your cause. Pitch them a story about how your activism relates to a current news event, and you may find a feature article in the newspaper to draw attention to the change you'd like to make.

People who can plan and conduct press conferences and write press releases will bring attention to the organization. Even individuals without a news background can write a letter to the editor, as I did for the first time in my life recently. It was much easier than I thought. Community members read letters to the editor; keep your issue in front of them.

Undercover Investigations and Whistleblowing

In 1906 Upton Sinclair wrote *The Jungle,* a fictional story based on the Chicago meatpacking industry. He exposed the terrible conditions of the industrial workers and the unsanitary conditions of the meat sent to consumers. His book led to changes in food industry standards.

Activists still try to expose problems existing outside the view of the public. Animal activists focus on this as a method because animals cannot tell their story; undercover activists work in slaughterhouses and document the cruel conditions there, on factory farms, and in the dairy industry. And they've gotten bold, daring the corporations to take actions against them, just to expose how animals are treated.[73]

Whistleblowing is revealing unethical acts in organizations. Famous whistleblowers include Sharron Watkins of ENRON, Jeffrey Wigand of the tobacco industry, and Mark Felt (a.k.a. Deep Throat) who exposed the Watergate scandal. More recently, the #MeToo movement has encouraged many sexual assault victims to come forward.

The Arts

The arts and activism sound strange together, but as I did my research, I found many examples of how artists use their skills for social justice. Rahwa Hammamy comments on how artivism does not look like protesting on the streets but is "...the creation of music and art that share truths that cannot be captured by words alone." [74]

Drawing and Illustration

At a recent protest, my husband entered the law enforcement screening area, and someone handed him this beautiful protest sign, a raised fist portrait, an homage to the 1968 Mexico City Olympics human rights salute by Americans Tommie Smith and Juan Carlos. A local artist used art for activism in a concrete way.

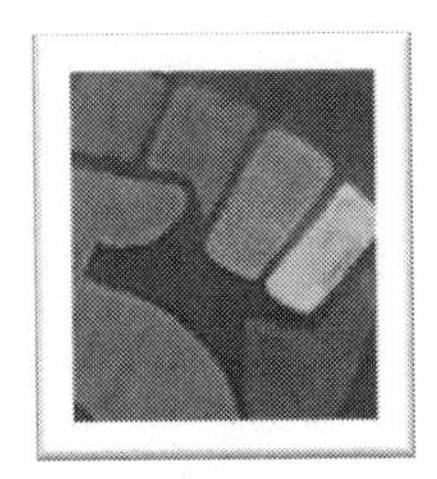

Using art for activism is not new. The drawing of a slave ship, *Stowage of the British Slave Ship Under the Regulated Slave Trade Act of 1788,* because of its terrible depiction of slaves lined up like sardines in a can, was instrumental in abolishing slavery.[75]

The use of a meme, word, phrase, or drawing easy to replicate and spread is typical. As a protest of Chinese government censorship of the Tiananmen Square pro-democracy protest, resisters changed the famous picture of the lone student facing down a column of tanks.[76] Instead of tanks, they inserted big yellow rubber duckies. After the meme went viral, the Chinese government banned the search term "big yellow duck." This led to other creative alternatives such as the Tiananmen Square Lego reenactment. These activists used their art to keep the cause alive in Chinese history.

Crafting

In Betsy Greer's books *Craftivism: The Art of Craft and Activism and Knitting for Good: A Guide to Creating Personal, Social, and Political Change Stitch by Stitch,* [77] I found many examples of crafters who used their gifts for their cause. Greer comments about the impact of an activist puppet show,

> *"I had always thought activism had to be loud and in-your-face. Maybe the quietness of the puppets resonated with the quietness of the knitting, but it made me think of quiet activism and wonder how craft could be a part of it."*

My favorite examples from Greer's book include the duo who knitted a Volkswagen bus and wore it while they walked through the streets of Belo Horizonte, Brazil to protest the lack of mass transit in the city. Also, the knitted mouse holding a sign saying "Down with Fat Cats" at the Occupy protest in front of St. Paul's Cathedral in London.

Greer says,

> *"Knitting means different things to different people. For some, it is simply a relaxing and productive hobby. For others, it may be any or all of the following: A way of expressing love and gratitude to a friend, a way of supporting individuals in need, a way of lessening the environmental impact of mass-produced goods, a way of protesting sweatshop labor, a way of making a livelihood, or a way of supplying needed household items. Whatever my reason for knitting, through the craft itself, I constantly have the opportunity to make profound statements about the ways in which I live."*

Activist Sarah Crockett uses craftivism to combine her love of stitch work with her concerns about the exploitation of garment workers. Before Sarah started this work, her activism experiences were loud and rowdy, usually an extrovert's knee-jerk reaction to an issue. As a strong introvert, this type of activism didn't match her needs.

In a campaign to urge a company to pay a living wage, she embroidered handmade handkerchiefs for each board member. The handkerchiefs, stitched with the words "Don't blow it," got her group in the door to pitch the living wage. Citing the unique campaign, the company yielded.

She trains activists to create opposition messages, put them in a beautiful package, and stash them in department store clothing for customers to find.

Corbett uses art for quiet activism, dropping scrolls in stores during fashion weeks. She says,

"I genuinely love fashion, and during fashion week there's a spotlight on the industry. I'd like to use that so we can think about how fashion could be beautiful on the inside as well as the outside." [78]

Documentaries and Films

What films or documentaries made an impact on you? When I was a young adult the movie *The Day After*, about the effects of nuclear war, gave me nightmares.

Documentaries and films use a progression of awareness, engagement, stronger movement, and finally change. [79]After viewing a movie, go to the film's website to learn more about the issues raised in the movie and what you can do to help.

Patricia Finneran, in her report *Documentary Impact: Social Change Through Storytelling* (on the use of documentary film for social change) says,

"Occasionally, and often to spectacular effect, a documentary lands in the public consciousness and launches a chain of events that can be seen to have changed society."[80]

She cites these films explicitly:

- ~ *Titicut Follies*, 1967 (mental hospital abuses)
- ~ *Hunger in America*, 1968 (poverty)
- ~ *Harlan County, USA*, 1976 (coal mining)
- ~ *An Inconvenient Truth*, 2006 (climate change)
- ~ *Food, Inc.*, 2008 (factory farming of animals)
- ~ *A Place at the Table*, 2012 (hunger)

~ *Made in L.A.*, 2013 (immigrant workers' rights)

Theater

The theater, like film, impacts social change by using a compelling story. It displays a live, three-dimensional message more powerful than movies because of the immediacy and intimate setting.

Lauri Golding reviewed the history of rhetoric and activism and describes the history of performance art with its roots in surrealism and its current incarnation of culture jamming.[81] The jamming part of the term comes from the history of interfering with radio broadcasts to allow unfiltered news to reach people. Today culture jamming is apparent in a variety of ways, from the satirical mockery of corporate logos to subversive ways to broadcast banned topics.

I was delighted to discover the 1960s guerrilla theatrical group *The Diggers*. They were actors in San Francisco who used their talents to imagine and present an ideal society and were an integral part of the Haight-Ashbury peace movement. But in addition to the theater, they fed folks in the park and opened a store where everything was free.

> *"The Diggers, as actors, created a series of street events that marked the evolution of the hippie phenomenon from a homegrown face-to-face community to the mass-media circus that splashed its face across the world's front pages and TV screens..."*[82]

A short segment of a larger film, *Tribute to the Summer of Love* (2017), features *The Diggers*.[83]

One of the most famous activist plays is Eve Ensler's *The Vagina Monologues*. Ensler followed the success of her play with the creation of V-Day, which focuses on ending violence against women and girls.[84]

Theater can influence even more if observers join into the performance. A creative approach called Legislative Theater involves skits depicting injustice; the actors perform the skit first, then a second time with invited legislators taking a role and trying to create a different outcome. Finally, the audience gets involved in the debate to discuss ways to right the injustices.[85]

Music

What social change music is on your playlist? I have iconic songs, such as John Lennon's *Imagine*, and one of my favorite albums is *So Far* by Crosby, Stills, Nash, and Young. Musicians can make an impact on social movements through their music. Over time musicians have used music to impact important issues:

- ~ Pete Seeger (labor movement, civil rights, anti-Vietnam War, environment)
- ~ Willie Nelson (Farm Aid)
- ~ John Lennon (world peace)
- ~ Bob Dylan (civil rights)
- ~ Joan Baez (civil rights, nonviolence, environment)
- ~ Bob Geldof (anti-poverty)
- ~ Bono (anti-poverty, Apartheid, AIDS)

Today, rap musicians increase awareness of racism and African American history and culture.[86]

Movement Support

In the same way leaders can help others use their strengths, those in movement support can take care of tasks for others. Supporting others in the movement can multiply the impact of the activism community.

Volunteer Care

This work supports most activism efforts. Caring includes feeding volunteers and giving comfort, so they don't have to worry about other areas of their life while they are helping your cause. In a more profound sense, the breaking of bread together is an opportunity for engagement in community. Small support gestures such as giving water on a sweltering day, making sure medical and support transportation are available, and just reminding another to "take ten" are meaningful.

Fundraising

Fundraising is essential work in activism efforts. The ability to develop community connections pays off in financial support for your organization, of course, but a great fundraiser uses those connections to build other forms of assistance. They understand a donor seeks a mutually dependent relationship and is likely to contribute eventually if they find it. Your organization will value these types of fundraising skills and connections.

Administrative Work

This work supports most activism efforts. Think about all the tasks required for an activism event, such as holding a forum for your cause. Although this is not the sexiest of activism jobs, the event would not happen without someone creating and duplicating educational materials, researching and scheduling space, arranging for food, setting up the microphone, and a multitude of tiny details that, done right, increase the odds of affecting your cause.

It's not Slacktivism: Activism for People with Limited Time

You want to make social change, but you also have a job, family, and limited time. If this is true, the following section highlighting quick activism is for you.

Social Media: Blogs and Podcasts/ Social Media Campaigns

The Internet has changed activism. Whether the change is directly related to making a difference in a cause is still unknown. But there is no denying the power of social media to make connections with like-minded others and to organize and implement social change activities. As Malcolm Gladwell says,

> *"The Internet lets us exploit the power of these kinds of distant connections with marvelous efficiency. It's terrific at the diffusion of innovation, interdisciplinary collaboration, seamlessly matching up buyers and sellers, and the logistical functions of the dating world."*[87]

A new term has arisen from the marriage of social media and activism—slacktivism. Slacktivism, a combination of slacker and activism, is a term that encompasses low-effort, low-risk activism opportunities such as signing an online petition, liking a Facebook page, and sharing activism posts. Some criticize slacktivism as lacking results or even harming causes. But research supports its impact.

One research study found participants who signed an online petition were more likely to donate money to a charity.[88] Other research showed success in using digital activism to draw public protests against the government, especially if the rule is authoritarian.[89] There was an increase in voting in response to social messaging.[90] However, we need to understand how best to use this tool for activism.[91]

Blogs that allow comments are helpful to engage others in a cause. It is a low-risk opportunity to express opinions and feel your viewpoint is heard.[92]

Lauri Goodling urges us to recognize digital activism:

> *As the variations of direct action begin to encompass new technologies, I would call on critics to reconsider their position on "slacktivism" and perhaps begin to see the value in the kinds of efforts that are being taken online. Rather than default to the pejorative variation, perhaps I could begin valuing "clicktivism." If I dismiss the notion of "feel good" passive activism—which is not unique to the digital age, by the way—and embrace the parallel efforts and expanded circulation afforded in the online world, I might be able to direct my focus to the education of Americans, particularly young Americans, on how to do this digital advocacy work effectively.*[93]

Go for it if you feel engaged, educated, and inspired.

Demonstrations/Protests/Direct Action

The 2017 Women's March on Washington was an uplifting experience, a top ten life experience for me. Because I had no cell phone coverage, I was unaware protestors were massing all over the world until I got back to my hotel and turned on the TV. More than five million people marched, the largest protest in history. I am so thankful to have been a part of it.

Protests and demonstrations are in-your-face activism. Their organizers hope to increase awareness and change public opinion. Persuasion research shows influence occurs when you appeal to the need for affiliation by highlighting what others are doing. A giant crowd of protesters is a concrete demonstration of what others believe about a cause.

Protests have been used throughout history to make a change. The Rev. Dr. Martin Luther King, Jr., following Gandhi's principles, espoused non-violence in the civil rights movement, specifically:

- ~ Non-violence is a way of life for courageous people.
- ~ Non-violence seeks to win friendship and understanding.
- ~ Non-violence seeks to defeat injustices, not people.
- ~ Non-violence holds that suffering for a cause can educate and transform.
- ~ Non-violence chooses love instead of hate.
- ~ Non-violence holds that the universe is on the side of justice and that right will prevail.[94]

Protests focused on one message and including large numbers of people are most likely to influence.[95] If many protests occur in an elected representative's district they are more likely to support civil rights.[96]

Corporate Protests

Corporate protests have increased, as activists use their buying power to advocate for change within companies. This has led businesses to see activist groups as stakeholders and to recognize their viewpoints in company decisions.[97]

For example, in response to the 2016 elections, a group called Sleeping Giants targeted the Breitbart News Network's bigotry by targeting organizations advertising on the Breitbart website. Nearly 2900 companies decided to defund Breitbart.[98] This has cratered their advertising income.

Shareholder activism

Shareholder activism is a form of a corporate boycott by those who own shares in the company. A bloc of shareholders voting together can influence the company to change policies and practices. A 1970 lawsuit challenging the legality of blocking social issues from a shareholder meeting agenda opened the door to allow protesters to push changes in business operations. Shareholder activists can impact social justice issues in the organization.[99]

Boycotts

Have you boycotted any products because of the producer's stance on an issue? To answer the question of whether boycotting products works—forces the manufacturer to make a change—Americus Reed writes,

"If the boycott reflects a movement — rather than a moment — it can change the world around it." [100]

Activists boycotted Nike because of labor practices, and the company changed its way of doing business with a strong focus on social justice. Many people boycotted Uber after their drivers "crossed the picket line" during the airport protest on Trump's immigration ban of seven predominately Muslim countries.

Corporate boycott success is magnified if the media covers the protest and works even better when the company has a less than stellar reputation at the time of the protest.[101]

Ethical Consumer publishes a list of current product and company boycotts but also encourages "the vote in your pocket," such as buying ethical products.[102]

Petitions

Petitions are floating around on many topics, and it is easy to take part in this type of activism. But are they effective? Although I did not find much research on whether they are effective, the website change.org includes a page called "Victories" highlighting successful petitions. The site also contains tools to create your own petitions for a cause you support.[103]

Divestment

Investors can choose socially responsible funds. These funds focus on organizations with ethical standards.

Activists are asking the New York City pension fund to divest from fossil fuel firms and invest in renewable energy firms. This type of protest has grown enough that investment companies are marketing socially responsible funds. Social responsibility encompasses a variety of issues, so know precisely what it means to you.

Go to Chapter 7 in *The WOYS? Workbook*

Talia's Story

Talia reviews the diverse types of activism methods. Certain methods she expected to motivate her didn't really light her fire. Lobbying was an example. On the other hand, several methods surprised her as being intriguing, such as coalition building. She found the idea of working with other people, teams, and organizations appeals to many motivators. She likes to work with others and believes it pushes her to perform better. She also values efficiency and wonders why organizations reinvent the wheel when they can work together and use each other's strengths.

Several methods were ones she had used before, such as boycotting and financial and administrative support. She remembers how much the small group she worked with appreciated her taking care of the finances so they could use the skills they enjoy. She didn't realize how much impact administrative support can make and how dire the need is for that sort of movement support.

She can support others trying to make behavioral change because of her work to help build financial capability. Members have praised her ability to draw out their needs and concerns and then help them find a way forward.

Talia's List of Activism Methods

- ~ Boycott
- ~ Coalition Building (but she's not ready for it yet)
- ~ Support programs (counseling for behavior change)
- ~ Administrative work (a surprise, but she knows she has the skills, and she now understands the potential impact)

Chapter Summary

Get motivated for activism by reviewing the myriad ways people have matched their skills with activism impact. From craftivists to kayaktivists, people are using their passions for change.

This chapter offers a broad variety of suggestions for activism work: running for office, lobbying, civil disobedience and sit-ins, volunteering and campaign management, fundraising, coalition building, educating others, research, art, crafting, music, theatre, and writing.

Those with limited time, money, or mobility explore slacktivism (the marriage of the Internet and activism). They get activism suggestions, including blogs, podcasts, and social media campaigns.

Every human is unique, but there are plenty of unique activism opportunities, too. Whatever your cause and skills, you will find something to motivate you. Having an idea of the methods used in activism means you can better match your gifts to the work.

In the next chapter, you will start to narrow your activism options.

CHAPTER 8

Narrow Your Activism Options

Each of us finds his unique vehicle for sharing with others his bit of wisdom.

~Ram Dass [104]

Objective

Choose your activism path.

Goal

Choose three to five activism opportunities to match your passions and gifts.

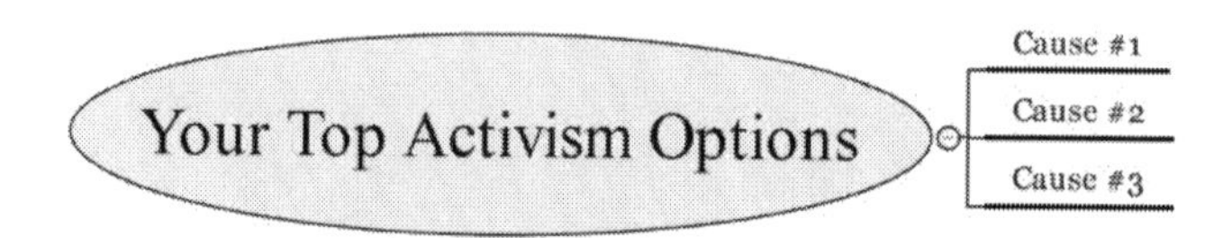

AS RAM DASS SAID IN HIS QUOTE at the beginning of this chapter, each of us finds a unique vehicle for sharing our wisdom with others. Understanding how to apply your skills and the opportunities you have in your cause may have led you to already find three to five activism choices to explore. That's great. If so, you can skip this chapter.

For some people, the match between their gifts and activism opportunities is easy to see, but I needed a process to find my match. Brainstorming ideas about how to best use my gifts yielded welcome results for me, ones I would have never unearthed without creative thinking.

What's On Your Sign?

In this chapter, you will choose the type of activism experiences that best suit you. Then you will narrow down your options. The work you've done so far will guide you in matching with activism opportunities.

Steps to Finding Activism Opportunities

1. Consider your passions (chapter 2)
2. Consider your skills (chapter 3)
3. Consider your motivation (chapter 4)
4. Consider the activism methods you like (chapter 5)
5. Brainstorm using charts to explore options (described in this chapter)
6. Brainstorm using Venn diagrams (described in this chapter)
7. Finalize your top three options

Included in this chapter are several methods for finding activism opportunities; use what works best for you, with the goal to find three to five areas to research further.

Brainstorming Your Activism Opportunities

Brainstorming is a creative process to generate ideas. The storming part of the name refers to letting ideas flow. Great ideas come from allowing freedom to create without evaluation. Here you will brainstorm with charts and Venn diagrams. Choose whatever feels comfortable for you or choose your own method. Just make sure you let your ideas flow.

Chart: Your Cause Matched With Your Skill Level

If you are sure of your cause and the skill you'd like to use, focus on your skill levels and what impact you can make on your cause. In the example below, the skill is Educating Others, and the cause is global warming. If you enjoy educating others and want to make an impact on the environment by reducing global warming, this table shows different options based on skill level.

Skill Level in Educating Others	Cause: Global Warming
Knowledge of topic but no experience as a teacher	Canvass for candidates with an environmental platform.
Have teaching skills	Teaching others about the impact of global warming and what they can do to reduce their carbon footprint.
Can design effective instruction	Prepare activist orientation training so volunteers can gain knowledge and skills and are ready for the cause sooner.
Have decent knowledge, instruction and influencing skills for educating others who are not receptive to the cause	Sit on a panel discussion about global warming that includes climate deniers.

Go to Chapter 8 in *The WOYS? Workbook*

Chart: Your Skill Level Matched with Activism Tasks

Another way to evaluate your prospects is to recognize different skills you can use in activism and your skill level in each. The higher your skill level, the more potential impact you can make. The chart below shows four basic activism skills and what task you can perform at each skill level.

Skill Level	Task: Writing	Task: Communicating
Basic	Preparing an event summary of several paragraphs	Answering the phone at campaign headquarters
Some experience	Preparing written materials on a unique topic	Explaining how to work a voting machine
Much experience	Preparing training manuals	Persuading others to vote for your candidate
Expert	Preparing research reports or original material	Leading negotiations on a new bill

Go to Chapter 8 in *The WOYS? Workbook*

Chart: Your Cause and Choice of Activism Methods

Another way to evaluate your activism opportunities is to reflect on your best skill and how to apply it to different tasks, as shown in the table below. People with specialized skills, such as attorneys, can use this approach.

If you are skilled in:	Cause: Racial Justice	Cause: Income Inequality
Influencing Others	Advocate for examination of different school discipline outcomes by race	Lobby for better consumer protection
Strategic Vision	Plan a campaign for a candidate to run for office	Plan a new software launch for lending circles
Educating Others	Create a documentary about race	Start an awareness day about equality
The Arts	Write a play about the experiences of immigrants	Draw a mural to illustrate wealth differences
News and Journalism Outreach	Research which journalists write about racial justice and develop relationships with them	Write letters to the editor about income inequality in your town
Sit-ins	Sit-in at your elected representative's office to support equality	Protest outside the hospital against the repeal of health insurance protections for low-income residents

Go to Chapter 8 in *The WOYS? Workbook*

Brainstorm Using Intersections

If you have multiple interests, look for the intersection of those interests to make a unique contribution.[105]

Richard Bolles, the author of *What Color is Your Parachute?* recommends this approach. The use of the overlapping circles (Venn diagrams) helps you analyze the intersection of your skills and interests. The intersection of three circles leads to creative options.

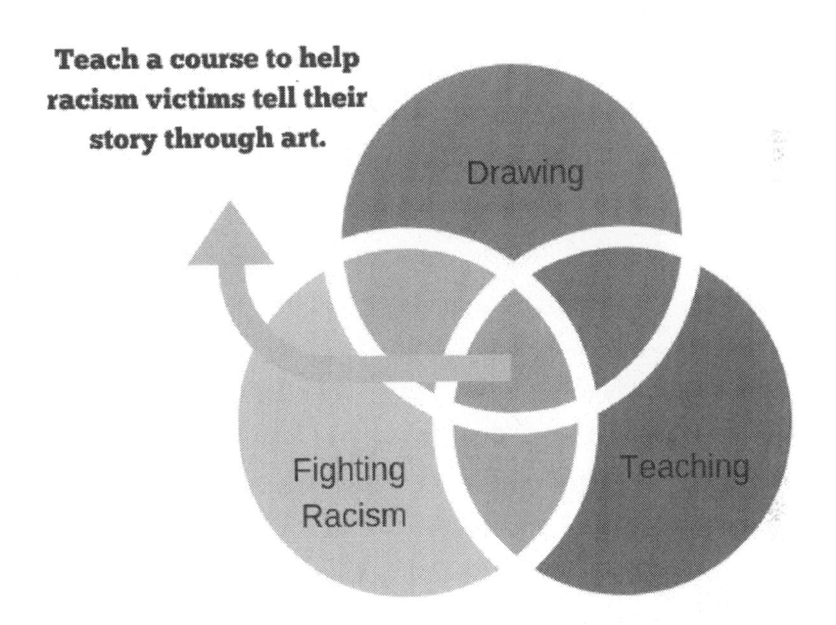

For example, if you want to work in teaching, racism prevention, and drawing, what work is possible for your cause? Perhaps you can teach a course on helping racism victims tell their stories through art.

Go to Chapter 8 in *The WOYS? Workbook*

Jim's Story

Jim knows what change he wants to make—more safe, affordable housing—but he has no idea how to start. He picks his top three skills, drawing, writing, and creativity, because he knows using them improves his odds of making an impact.

Skill Level	*Skill 1: Drawing*	*Skill 2: Writing*	*Skill 3: Creativity*
Basic			
Some Experience		Has written copy for some marketing campaigns	
Many Experiences			Using creativity has been part of all his jobs
Expert	Works as a graphic designer		

Completing the chart reminds him of his drawing ability and how essential the arts are to his life. Jim contacts a local activist organization and asks if they have need of a volunteer graphic designer. The organization's director invites Jim to meet with her to brainstorm ideas. Together, they come up with a visual ad campaign focused on the upcoming rehab of the city's affordable housing developments. They design the campaign to encourage the city council to adopt green standards in the rehab. Jim's drawings feature residents enjoying apartments with natural-gas hot water heaters and a solar panel roof system. The images communicate the advantages of green updates in a clear, concise way and the city council votes to go ahead with the idea.

Talia's Story

Talia reviewed the results of the work she'd done so far. She knew her top skills, her knowledge, and her motivation for activism. She also knew which activism methods were attractive to her.

A skill Talia would like to use is organizing, so she used a chart to examine her skill level. Talia believed she is at expert level in the skill of organizing herself and others.

Skill Level	*Organizing*
Basic	Organizing work that doesn't need coordination with others
Some experience	Coordinating some of your work with others
Much experience	Adjusting the order in which tasks are done, or rescheduling tasks or workers
Expert	Organizing your and others' work

Next Talia considered a chart to help her brainstorm ideas for using her skills in areas she is passionate about.

Skill	*Cause: Income Inequality*	*Cause: Disability Awareness*	*Cause: Animal Activism*
Organization	Planning tax workshops	Organizing a support program to highlight disability awareness	Canvass restaurants to add vegan options to their menu
Support & Counseling	Helping with financial capability	Helping parents with IEPs	Helping with switching to a vegan diet
Movement Support	Organizing training classes on financial capability	Moderating a forum about disability awareness	Handling finances for the animal shelter
Boycott	Boycotting drug companies to protest price increases	Protesting the school board	Boycotting cruel products

Finally, Talia brainstormed using intersections.

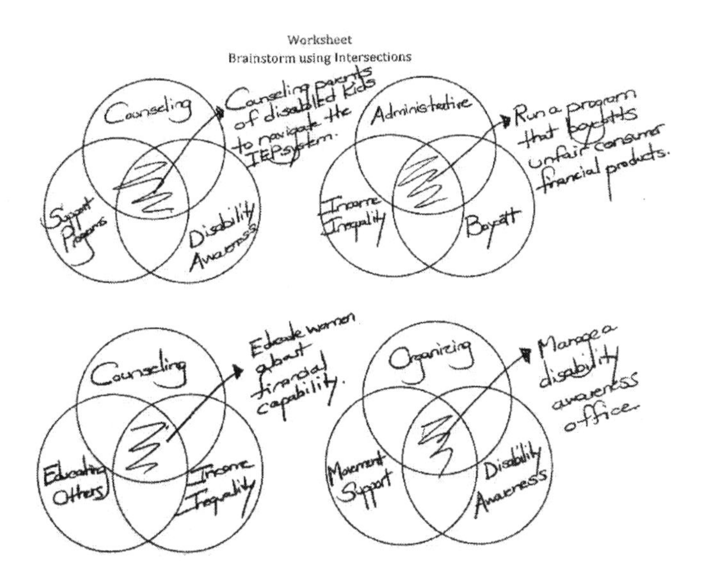

Talia enjoyed brainstorming ideas and found three areas she felt are reasonable matches between her gifts and her passion for change:

~ Manage an office for one of her causes.

~ Counsel parents of kids with disabilities on how to get services.

~ Help women gain financial capability.

Chapter Summary

Pull your previous work together into the best match between your gifts and activism opportunities.

Evaluate what you've learned about yourself thus far to begin to narrow down your choices of activism work. Consider:

- ~ Passions (chapters 1 and 2)
- ~ Skills and knowledge (chapters 3 and 4)
- ~ Motivation (chapter 5)
- ~ Ideal activism opportunity (chapter 6)
- ~ Activism methods (chapter 7)

You have a clearer picture of yourself and what you bring to activism, as well as what you want to do. If you already know your cause, use a Skills Level chart to match it with your skill levels. If you have an expert skill, pair it with activism tasks or causes. You will use your top two or three choices in the next chapter.

Jim and Talia use brainstorming to narrow down their activism opportunities to those matched to their skills, knowledge, and motivation. Jim loves the arts and puts it to use for a cause important to him. Talia is less certain about her ability but finds many options for her activism.

Having a good fit with your work is important in employment and activism. It may not be easy to narrow down your opportunities, but I hope you were able to find three to five activism opportunities to match your passions and gifts.

In the next chapter, you will make sure your activism opportunities will have an impact.

Activist in Action: Summer Awad

Don't let anyone tell you that your story is not for the stage, and don't let anyone tell you that you can't change minds and hearts through performance art. ~ Summer Awad

Growing up as a Palestinian American in East Tennessee, I knew from a young age that I was different. My exposure to Arabic and Islam and my experiences with my family did not align with the stereotypes and hatred against Arab Muslims after 9/11. I felt drawn to politics and activism early because I saw the harm caused by discrimination.

Since elementary school, I acted in plays, joined school dance teams, and competed in poetry recitation contests. I was always moved by stage performance and felt comfortable in front of an audience. In college, after landing a role in a production of *The Vagina Monologues* by Eve Ensler, I started to see the possibilities of what theatre could do. I had been accustomed to traditional Shakespeare plays or musicals with largely white, heterosexual casts. Because of *The Vagina Monologues,* I realized that theatre could take whatever form one wanted it to take.

At the same time, I was building community with other students of Palestinian descent and learning for the first time what it meant to be descended from the victims of violent settler colonialism. As I studied Arabic, a lifelong goal of mine, my interests in theatre, personal heritage, and Palestinian human rights merged perfectly. I decided to write a play as my culminating senior thesis project for my self-designed major in Literary Activism.

With the resources of the theatre and Arabic departments at UT and an outpouring of support from the community, "WALLS: A Play for Palestine" was born. Over 400 people attended the premiere at the Clarence Brown LAB Theatre, and we were later accepted to the New York International Fringe Festival.

Through the writing and production of this play, I learned so much about teamwork in theatre production, as well as the importance of telling overlooked and authentic stories on the stage. Often, an issue that people think of as too complicated or political is best illuminated by creating and presenting relatable characters.

In WALLS, Diaspora Child struggles in her relationship with her conservative Muslim father while learning about the historical struggles of Palestinians. The universal father-daughter narrative and the typical struggles of second-generation immigrants help lighten the mood of a heavy political story. This medium proved to be successful for audiences who are new to the issue of Palestine.

I often like to quote Toni Morrison: "If there is a book you want to read but it hasn't been written yet, then you must write it." I would encourage political artists to carve out a space for themselves in places where they may not have been represented before. Don't let anyone tell you that your story is not for the stage, and don't let anyone tell you that you can't change minds and hearts through performance art. My experience has been a testament to the contrary.

Summer Awad is a Knoxville native of Palestinian descent. You can learn more about her play at http://wallsplay.com. Summer works as a case manager with Bridge Refugee Services, the local refugee resettlement affiliate. She graduated from the University of Tennessee in 2016 with a degree in Literary Activism. In addition to being a playwright, Summer is an activist and spoken word artist, performing under the stage name "Uncensored." She is involved with the Knoxville City Council Movement and performs as a vocalist in the University of Tennessee Middle East Ensemble.

PART 4

Your Activism Choice

In Part 4 focus on ensuring that your activism choice makes the most impact possible for your cause. Research and choose your ideal activism opportunity.

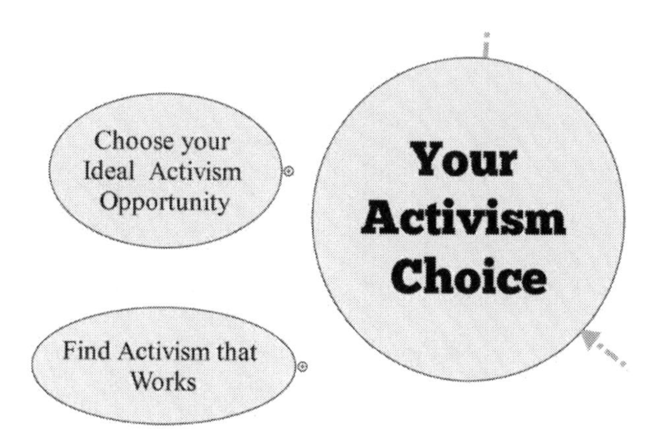

Part 4 includes:

Chapter 9: Find Activism That Works

Chapter 10: Choose Your Ideal Activism Opportunity

CHAPTER 9

Find Activism That Works

When it comes to helping people, being unreflective often means being ineffective. ~William MacAskill [106]

Objective

Find potential activism opportunities that make a positive impact on your cause.

Goal

Analyze your potential activism opportunities to decide if they make a positive impact on your cause.

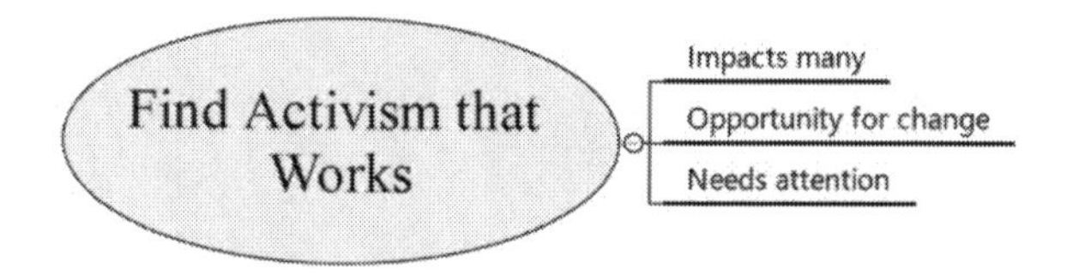

I HOPE YOUR EXAMINATION OF YOUR passions, anger, love, and heartbreak led you to pinpoint themes for your activism. You may have recognized a calling. You have a life plan in place. Getting focused on your passion is a good start to finding your best activism opportunity. By the time you finish Part 4, you will pick an activism method to make a real impact on your cause.

You will devote a significant amount of your time to activism, so you want to know you are making a difference. But evaluating social justice impact is not easy, and so it's neglected even by professional nonprofits; it's difficult to find the real effect of an organization's work. But as Milton Friedman said, "One of the great mistakes is to judge policies and programs by their intentions rather than their results."[107]

Effective Altruism

Do you know the impact of your charitable donations? You've seen the commercials. Eyes glistening, the puppy gazes at the camera with a "Don't let me die here" expression. If you don't send in $1.50 a month, that's less than the cost of one coffee, by the way, little Fido is doomed. The advertisement tugs at your heart and purse strings.

How are we supposed to quit opening our wallet for every dewy-eyed commercial spokesperson or animal?

Two steps.

Step 1: Be sure about your values and choose an issue important to you. Then, every time you see a commercial or folks knock on the door, or your employer asks for automatic deductions from your paycheck for the United Way, you say no. If you want to elaborate, tell them about your cause. If you are feeling cheeky, ask them for money.

Step 2: Once you know your issue, find a charity that makes the best use of your donation.

A movement called effective altruism evaluates charities to ensure donations dramatically improve a vast number of lives, make a significant change, and contribute to overlooked causes.

It makes sense to want your donations to affect many lives. But certain charities have less impact than others. For example, look at animal activism.

Remember Fido? Animal suffering is undoubtedly worthy of being alleviated because in the US about three million dogs and cats are killed in shelters every year. But compare this to the nine billion chickens and tens of millions of pigs and cows killed in factory farms. We can change many more lives by supporting charities to save factory-farmed animals.

Effective altruists also evaluate the charity's ability to make change. Within a cause, certain charities make more difference than others. For example, giving anti-malarial bed nets offers 500 times the benefit of treating the disease.

Finally, effective altruists recognize how much a cause is neglected. Charities in poorer countries are underfunded because citizens of wealthy nations tend to donate locally. Our money may go much farther if sent overseas.

The effective altruism websites Givewell.org and effectivealtruism.org help you choose charities that dramatically improve a vast number of lives, make a significant change, and focus on overlooked causes. They vet the charity and calculate the impact for you.

To recap, Step 1: Identify the charitable cause most important to you. Step 2: Find the most effective charities for your cause and send them money.

Now relax, knowing you maximized the donation impact for an issue you care about. And if you switch on the TV and see a dewy-eyed puppy beseeching you with a "Don't let me die here" expression, don't send in $1.50 a month, even though it's less than the cost of one coffee. You are good.

Effective Activism

I've taken this detour to effective altruism because we can apply the ideas to effective activism. For example, here are the effective altruism criteria reworked to focus on effective activism:

~ Will the activism dramatically improve a large number of lives?
~ How much change can you make?
~ How much is the cause overlooked?

You can use these questions to decide if your activism focus is effective.

William MacAskill, the author of the book *Doing Good Better*, recommends the use of effective altruism criteria for effective activism, with one addition. He adds personal fit as a criterion, "given your skills, resources, knowledge, connections, and passions, how likely are you to make a large difference in this area?"[108]

Adding the question about personal fit, which is what you've been working on already in this book, you have four questions:

~ Will the activism dramatically improve a large number of lives?
~ How much change can I make?
~ How much is the cause overlooked?
~ Will my skills and passions lead to making a difference?

Use these questions to figure out whether your activism focus is effective.

Linda's Story

Right after the Charlottesville murder of activist Heather Heyer, a white supremacist group applied for a rally permit near a Civil War statue in Linda's town. Less than 20 white supremacists showed up, but more than 3000 counter-protesters were there, including Linda, her husband, and her son. It wasn't an easy decision to go to the protest in the wake of the Charlottesville violence. But she decided, as a white person, she must stand up against white supremacy. Her city government and law enforcement handled the protest well. No one was hurt, and police only arrested one protester, for not giving up a mason jar (a uniquely Southern problem). Law enforcement kept the groups separated. Thousands waited with protest signs, and Linda laughed when just a few white supremacists showed up on the other side of the street. Linda and her family left early, feeling as if the counter-protest was a success.

Let's look at Linda's activism efforts using the effective activism criteria.

Will the activism dramatically improve a large number of lives?

Linda's participation in the rally likely didn't impact any lives. It made her glad she had stood up for racial justice. But if she hadn't shown up would it have made a difference? Probably not. Linda posted pictures online to let her Facebook friends know the counter-protest was going well and that made some of them happy. It made a few of her Facebook friends unhappy because they wish she would stay out of potentially dangerous situations like this may have been. Overall estimate = 0 lives impacted.

How much change can I make?

What change was the goal of the counter-protest? Linda's goal was to counter racist attitude in her area with support for racial justice. Showing up for those who don't have her privilege is vital to her. But did the counter-protest change attitudes toward racism in her city? Probably not. And one of the problems with this type of activism is there is no measure of whether it worked or not. No one came behind and surveyed those who witnessed the counter-protest or watched the news reports. Overall estimate of change = Low.

How much is the cause overlooked?

Racial justice is not a neglected area of social change. In fact, in the time after Charlottesville, it dominated the news. Racial justice has been a focus for decades, and there has been progress, but unfortunately, populism has fanned the issue into flame again. That has increased the focus on the issue compared to pre-2017. Linda may argue that participation by white people in racial justice needs more attention but other organizations in her area are working on the issue. Overall estimate of whether the cause is neglected = Low.

Will my skills and passions lead to making a difference?

This was not a personal fit regarding Linda's wish for quiet, no crowds, and safety. But because of her passion for racial justice, it was a match with her values and hopes for her community. There are other areas of racial justice activism Linda can pursue to create more impact. Overall estimate of personal fit leading to change = Low.

Linda's Story

Linda decided to look for more impactful ways of promoting racial justice in her community. She is a teacher, and she knew from years of experience that teachers are not well prepared to answer questions students ask them about race. Her students were asking more questions since the election, and she checked around to see if this was true for her fellow teachers.

During a grade level planning meeting she spoke up. She verified her fellow teachers were hearing more questions about race and wished to handle them better, too. Linda suggested a teacher and parent community training session.

Let's look at Linda's new activism effort using the effective activism criteria.

Will the activism dramatically improve a large number of lives?

Linda's forum has the potential to impact her school's 15 teachers and

233 students and their families. Linda plans and holds the community forum. Afterward, she sends a short evaluation questionnaire to the teachers and parents/guardians, and after three months, surveys the students. Teachers rated the session as highly effective. Parent attendance was 10%, and they also rated the forum as highly effective. Students showed an increase in number of questions answered from pre-forum to post-forum. Overall estimate = approximately 335 lives impacted.

How much change can I make?
What change was the goal of Linda's activism? Linda's goal was to counter racist attitude in her area with support for racial justice. She focused on helping teachers and parents talk with their kids about race. Her forum evaluation showed students were more likely to have discussions with parents and teachers about race. Overall estimate of change = Low, although Linda believes it is a start.

How much is the cause overlooked?
Racial justice is not a neglected area of social change, but Linda's focus is unique to her community. Other sources of information are available online, but Linda's forum provides actual practice and role modeling to better ensure skill building. Overall estimate of whether the cause is neglected = High.

Will my skills and passions lead to making a difference?
This effort was a personal fit for Linda because of her passion for racial

justice, her teaching skills, and her motivation to make a difference for the kids in her classroom. Overall estimate of personal fit leading to change = High.

Linda's work started in her grade level and expanded to the entire school. The evaluation showed evidence of the impact and the whole school system adopted the program. Linda is now consulting with other systems to implement the program in their schools.

Go to Chapter 9 in *The WOYS? Workbook*

Activism Choice Grid

The Activism Choice Grid is based on the effective altruism criteria. Use the grid to evaluate your activism opportunities.

Choose three activism ideas and enter them into the grid.

For each idea you have listed, rank order them for each criterion.[109] Use 1 for the best choice for you and 3 for the worst option for you.

Criteria	Idea 1	Idea 2	Idea 3
Lives impacted			
Potential for change			
Needs attention			
Personal fit for my skills			
Personal fit for my knowledge			
Personal fit for my motivation			
TOTAL			

Following the ranking process, add up your scores. The lowest ranked cause is the one most suitable for you.

If you have a distinct winner, great! If not, use the top two choices for further research.

Go to Chapter 9 in *The WOYS? Workbook*

Talia's Story

Talia prioritizes her choices of managing an office for one of her causes, teaching parents of disabled students how to get services, and helping women gain financial capability.

Criteria	*Manage an office for one of her causes*	*Teach parents IEP navigation*	*Help women gain financial capability*
Lives impacted	1	2	3
Potential for change	1	3	2
Needs attention	2	3	1
Personal fit for my skills	2	3	1
Personal fit for my knowledge	2	3	1
Personal fit for my motivation	1	3	2
TOTAL	9	17	10

Talia's top choice according to the grid is managing an office for one of her causes, with helping women gain financial capability coming in a close second.

To gain more information about her choice she used Clearer Thinking's Decision Advisor. This online tool helps you see options and prompts you to avoid common problem-solving errors.

Clearer Thinking's Decision Advisor Tool Results

	Manage a non-profit	***Help women gain financial capability***
Leaning toward		x
Advantages	"I would impact more lives." "I can learn new skills." "Less time-consuming."	"I have these skills." "Working directly with clients."
Disadvantages	"Less interaction with clients." "Less direct impact from my skills."	"I already do this in my job." "I want to learn new skills."
Final choice	x	
	You became substantially more confident in your choice during your reflections. Your confidence increased by 30%.	

Talia's Decision Advisor results reinforced "managing an office for one of her causes" as the top choice.

Talia was satisfied with her evaluation of her activism opportunities and was ready to start finding the right place for her.

Although most of McCaskill's book is focused on effective altruism, he provides his results from using the effective altruism criteria for activism choices. See if these resonate with you and match your personal fit:

- ~ US Criminal justice reform—rates of incarceration are high and don't appear to deter crime.
- ~ International labor mobility—reducing barriers to labor force mobility to move from one country to another for work.
- ~ Factory farming —cruel and terrible for the environment.
- ~ 2 to 4-degree climate change—this small change in global temperature will have an enormous impact on many lives. Focused mostly on reducing emissions.
- ~ Catastrophic climate change—a catastrophic change in global temperatures. Neglected, compared to reducing emissions. Research in geoengineering (ways to cool the Earth).
- ~ Other global catastrophic risks—unlikely but devastating threats such as nuclear war, bioterrorism, and pandemics.[110]

Phew, that's a bit overwhelming, isn't it? But I ended up focusing on one of these MacAskill areas in my activism. And as just one individual in the fight, I matched up my personal fit against what I'm passionate about and know I'm working on a cause I can impact. I won't make a difference by myself, but I know I am doing what I can.

Chapter Summary

Effective altruism focuses on helping people make the most impact with their charitable donations. Use a similar process to figure out how you can make the most impact with your activism work, a process known as effective activism.

Here are the effective altruism criteria reworked to focus on effective activism:

- Will the activism dramatically improve a large number of lives?
- How much change can you make?
- How much is the cause overlooked?
- Will my skills and passions lead to making a difference?

You can use these questions to maximize the impact of your activism.

If you are passionate about a cause, take the extra time to evaluate whether the work you are doing is making an impact. Then check to see if there are more effective activism methods.

The story of Linda shows the need to evaluate activism work, so your efforts pay off in change. As William MacAskill says, "When it comes to helping people, being unreflective often means being ineffective." Taking the time to reflect means you can make more impact.

In the next chapter, you will gather information and make a choice for your activism.

CHAPTER 10

Choose Your Ideal Activism Opportunity

You must be the change you wish to see in the world.
~Mahatma Gandhi [111]

Objective

Choose and plan the start of your ideal activism.

Goal

Prepare to begin your ideal activism.

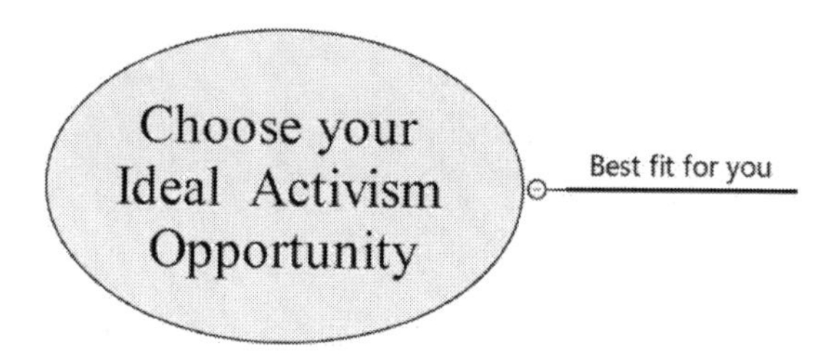

IN THE LAST CHAPTER, YOU RANKED your activism choices in the Activism Choice Grid and picked one or two to research further. Study the methods and the organization you are considering. Applicants for paid positions should do this; I can tell you from sitting on the hiring side of the desk I'm impressed when a candidate asks excellent questions about an organization and makes it obvious they've studied the company.

Today's access to information also means you have more than just the official data provided by the organization. "Applicants have a lot of outside sources available at the click of a mouse (or the touch of a phone!) to make their evaluations—news stories, reviews on Glassdoor, social media posts, and insight from friends, relatives, or friends of friends who are current or previous employees."[112]

Self-Education

When you choose your activism area at the end of this process, you must educate yourself about your cause. If you have chosen something you are passionate about, this education will motivate you. For example, if you are interested in influencing others to vote for your candidate, educate yourself about the person and his or her platform. Make sure you have the information you need to make an informed vote and be ready to answer others' questions.

Libraries

I remember the ways I had to find information before the Internet. Libraries were the go-to source for information in those days, and although I have the Internet now, libraries are still one of my favorite places. I love browsing the New Releases section to see what sparks my interest. I know which parts of the Dewey Decimal System focus on my interests. Skilled reference librarians help you with your questions.

In an essay about teaching English to college students, Tegan Bennett Daylight's last goal for her students resonates with me, "Finally, I want them to see that reading breeds thinking, and thinking breeds resistance, and surely, especially right now, that is a good thing."[113]

The written word has long been used for activism. Lauri Goodling reviewed the history of rhetoric and activism, which includes zines and alternative journalism. Today activists are using technology for citizen journalism as an alternative to mainstream media.

Fact-Check

To ensure you have reputable information about your cause:

~ Recognize the reputation of the sources you choose to use regularly. Try to focus on the unbiased ones and avoid those reporting from a biased position.

~ Make sure the sources you are not familiar with are reputable.

- Look for data to check assertions. I like this comprehensive resource provided by Howard Rheingold, *A Guide to Crap Detection Resources*, to help me decide what information is truthful and unbiased. It includes tools to check websites, social media, academic sources, and political sources. For example, in the section "Political" there are links to resources such as Project Vote Smart, which makes information about public officials available.[114]
- Check the URL of the source. If you are looking for information about the State of Missouri, your URL is https://www.mo.gov/government/. A fake site is almost identical, but with one small change that you are unlikely to see: https://www.mo.com/government.

- Check quotes or images to see if they are legitimate. Copy and paste them into Google.

~ Read or listen to reputable sources aligned with your causes and values.

Identify and Research Potential Organizations

There are many sources to help you identify potential organizations for your activism work. When you find an organization that interests you, dive into the tools presented in this section to research the organization. Get the information you need to make a good decision.

Online Information

Charity evaluators

Charity evaluators from the effective altruism movement are excellent sources of information for identifying and researching potential organizations. An excellent source is Give Well.

An organization's official website

The organization's official website is a suitable place to start. Look for their mission statement. Look at the organization's job postings and volunteer opportunities; are the skills they are seeking a match for yours? See if national groups working on the issue have a local chapter. What foundations are supporting the cause? Researching a national organization may provide you with more information than is available for a local group.

Background Information

For example, if you are interested in supporting a politician, find the listing of how he or she has voted on specific issues.

Online courses

These are available for many knowledge and skill areas and are mostly free. Use these for self-education about your cause (or create one yourself to promote your cause). Examples include Coursera and FutureLearn.

Databases

Check out databases, such as VolunteerMatch.org and www.idealist.org.

Websites to Research Organizations

You can get insider information by checking out the organization on www.LinkedIn.com and www.GlassDoor.com.

Newsletters and Blogs

As you are browsing, sign up for newsletters and blogs to help you learn about the organization.

Online Groups

Look online for groups talking about your issue. Where are they doing their activism?[115]

Google Alerts

Use information-gathering tools such as Google Alerts.

Your Support Network

Personal Suggestions

Check with other activists for their recommendations on the best resources to get started.

Word of Mouth Networking

Who can you speak with about the cause? Keep track of useful contacts if you decide to go further with the organization.

Go to Chapter 10 in *The WOYS? Workbook*

A Concise Statement of your Cause: Your Elevator Speech

A tool I am borrowing from the paid work world is the elevator speech. An elevator speech is an idea you want to sell in 30-60 seconds. Imagine you are a new, low-level employee working in a multinational organization's headquarters in a high-rise building. You are on the elevator with the CEO and have a minute to pitch yourself and an idea. You must catch her attention and sell her on why it's a great idea and, of course, why you are the right one to implement it.

To create your activism elevator speech, picture the person you are pitching and put yourself in their shoes. Talk about why you care. As Gandhi says, "Be the change you want to see in the world."

Here is an example of an activism elevator speech, from Adam, a teenage animal activist:

In my family, we love our pets and make sure they are happy. One day in elementary school a kid mentioned pigs are like dogs; they are smart and sociable and feel emotions. I was eating a BLT at the time, and I imagined eating my dog, Scarlet. I felt sick to my stomach. I have healthier food choices, so I choose not to eat animals. I made the decision to eat only plants 10 years ago. When I started high school, I began advocating for more plant-based meals in my school cafeteria. They have reduced egg

> *consumption by 40% and agreed to use only free-range eggs. I hope someday we eat only plants in school cafeterias.*

In your activism search, you will use the elevator speech to let others know about your cause and what you want to accomplish. When you are finally working on your cause, your elevator speech will help you recruit others, fundraise, and lobby.

Create your elevator speech and practice on a few people. Incorporate their feedback.

Go to Chapter 10 in *The WOYS? Workbook*

Get Feedback about Your Cause from an Activist

When you have an idea of areas for your activism, ask for a sit-down conversation with an activist working in your potential activism area. This is an information-gathering discussion to help you learn about the activist's development in the work and potentially get contacts and leads for your research. You will use your elevator speech to get this appointment.

Your goal is to find out more about working as an activist.

Consider using the following questions, or create your own:

- ~ What were experiences essential to your development?
- ~ How did you learn these things?
- ~ What advice do you have for me?
- ~ How did you make sure you were prepared to work with people who are different than you?

- Did you encounter any areas where you were unprepared? How did that inform your activism?
- What skills and knowledge do I need to help the cause?
- Do you have anyone I should talk to?

Write a thank you note to the person who gave up their valuable time to help you.

Go to Chapter 10 in *The WOYS? Workbook*

What you Need to Know about Your Organization

I am talking about you choosing the organization. You control this search.

In the past, you may have picked an organization, contacted them, and had them sign you up on the spot. The best choice is not an organization that signs you up without question. Effective organizations are thoughtful about how they recruit, develop, and mobilize volunteers.

Besides, you need an opportunity to find out:

- what the position is like
- whether it is a satisfactory match for you
- how the organization is living the written mission statement
- the ways it cares for its volunteers
- the day-to-day duties of the position
- the best and worst parts of the work
- how much you can negotiate the terms of your service

- the contact number of activists so you can check their experiences

You need to get information if the organization isn't perceptive enough to provide it. If they have something like a Realistic Job Preview, that's a positive sign. They take their volunteers and organization seriously and know a match is essential to prevent volunteer turnover. If they don't have something formal, you must get that information.

It is also crucial for you to negotiate your activism terms. Remember, this is not self-centered. It is realistic and helpful to both you and the organization. Understand the hours expected and whether it matches your wishes. What level of responsibility do you want? Make it obvious.

Before you leave the discussion, get contact information for a few other activists you can talk with separately. This is the activism-hunting version of reference checking. Do these volunteers have a positive experience? How are they making an impact? Is the organization treating them well?

Another reason to have contact information is to take advantage of shadowing an activist. This involves following her around as she does her activism work, so you can get a real sense of the work and working conditions. One study in a nursing setting found job shadowing was related to lower stress, higher job performance, and more positive attitudes about the company. [116] Practices such as job shadowing, coaching, and mentoring impact employees' beliefs that the organization lives up to its promises. Consequently, they were more satisfied and less likely to leave.[117]

Use your contacts and support network to find the right person and schedule a discussion. Since full-time activists are busy, prepare well so you get the information you need and convey what you want about yourself efficiently.

Ready Yourself: Set a Goal for Your Organizational Meeting

All right – go out and interview someone in the organization!

What just came to mind when you read that sentence? Did the thought of starting scare you?

Tara Mohr aims her recommendations in *Playing Big* at women, who she noticed in her coaching work seemed reluctant to act on their excellent ideas. But I believe her suggestions are useful for anyone hesitating about starting something new. I admit, Mohr describes ways I put off getting started – by working on my plan to the nth degree but never actually implementing it, and by using excuses such as not enough time and lack of the proper credentials to do something I am perfectly capable of doing.[118]

Recognize when you are critical of yourself rather than supportive. Is your inner voice tearing you down or building you up?

If you recognize yourself in Mohr's descriptions, I recommend you read her book. She will help you with your activism but, more importantly, it will help you with your life.

Stepping out of my comfort zone is hard. Fortunately, there have been several mentors in my life who recognized my abilities even when I had doubts.

As President Jimmy Carter said, "You can do what you have to do, and sometimes you can do it even better than you think you can." [119]

Address your resistance

By the time you've completed this entire self-assessment, you may feel empowered and ready to go. If so, skip to Part 5. But if you have hesitation, stay here, and I will dissolve your uncertainties.

You addressed your own questions about capability with your self-assessment process because you picked a cause you feel confident about and motivated to support. You will have to learn and make changes along the way, but trust you are on the right path for you.

Set a Goal for the Discussion

Setting goals means better performance. Goals focus your effort, so you work on the right activities. If those goals are moderately difficult, you are more motivated. Finally, by adding feedback about your performance, you have a recipe for success.

Goal setting works and is used all over the world. You must set goals. Let's take the extra step to use a more scientific approach - SMART goals.[120]

The SMART acronym stands for specific, measurable, achievable, relevant, and timely.

SMART

Specific	Be clear about the behavior you will perform
Measurable	Make it specific and measurable
Achievable	Make sure your behavior can be achieved, is realistic
Relevant	Ensure your behavior moves you forward in your cause
Timely	List when will you perform this action

Don't be like Douglas Adams, who said,

"I love deadlines. I like the whooshing sounds they make as they fly by."[121]

Create a plan to guide your focus.

Your next step is to have a discussion with an activist from the organization for which you want to volunteer. Here is an example of using a SMART goal.

Specific - be very clear about the action you will perform.	Sit down with the director of Refugee Services to find out about opportunities.
Measurable - how will you know you have accomplished it?	I get the information I need from the director.
Achievable - make sure your action can be achieved, is realistic.	Yes. I've done a lot of work on my self-assessment and research.
Relevant - does this action move you forward in your cause?	This is the cause I'm most interested in so I want to make sure it is a fitting match.
Timely – when will you perform this action?	I will schedule it within a week and hope to have the discussion within 2 weeks.

You'll set SMART goals as part of starting in your cause, too.

Go to Chapter 10 in *The WOYS? Workbook*

Your Discussion with a Leader from the Organization

Prepare for the discussion by:

- ~ Being clear on what information you want from this person.
- ~ Prepare to use excellent active listening skills. Follow up if the person gets off track and doesn't answer your question. Use techniques to redirect them to the information you want.
- ~ Practice conducting the discussion with a friend beforehand.

The Interview

Introduce yourself using your elevator speech. Describe the purpose of the discussion. For example, to ask questions about the organization and activism opportunity, to hear about the work they do, and to answer any questions they have about you.

Consider using the following questions:

- ~ I know your mission is...How do you live this in your work?
- ~ Where is the most need for support right now?
- ~ How do you organize volunteers and the work?
- ~ Describe a typical way you find a match between a person's skills and motivations and the work that needs to be done.

- I'm guessing that occasionally volunteers are dissatisfied. Tell me about the most challenging volunteer you have had to deal with. Was the volunteer satisfied at the end?
- How do you evaluate the success of your work?
- Tell me about how you support and care for volunteers.
- Tell me about a typical day for your volunteers. What's good? What's hard?
- Are you willing to provide me with contact information for a few activists I might talk to about the work?

If you are quite interested in the opportunity, consider these questions:

- This is what I'd like to do. Would it be possible for me to begin volunteering here? Do you have comments or questions about what I have to offer?
- What do you need from me before I get started with this work?

Go to Chapter 10 in *The WOYS? Workbook*

Checking in with a Volunteer from the Organization

After your discussion, if you want to pursue the opportunity, check with the volunteer activists using this template:

Introduce yourself using your elevator speech. Describe the purpose of the call – "I'm interested in doing activism work with XYZ organization, and I wanted to check in with a volunteer, to make sure it is the right place for me."

Consider using these questions:

- ~ Are/were you happy with the activism you do?
- ~ If yes, describe some of the reasons why.
- ~ If no, why not?
- ~ What is your overall assessment of the organization?
- ~ Would you recommend I give this organization a try?
- ~ How do they match your skills and motivation with the work?
- ~ How do they care for and support volunteers?
- ~ How do they help you develop as an activist?
- ~ Are there additional comments you'd like to make?

Go to Chapter 10 in *The WOYS? Workbook*

Your Choice

Make your decision and look forward to making change.

Talia's Story

Identify Potential Organizations

Talia began her search by looking for potential organizations. Specifically, she wanted to apply her financial skills to a cause she supports.

She started with the effective altruism websites because third parties vet and verify their effectiveness.

One charity, Give Directly, supported a cause she is interested in – helping bolster poor families with direct financial help. She looked at their mission:

> *GiveDirectly was founded by Paul Niehaus, Michael Faye, Rohit Wanchoo and Jeremy Shapiro, who were studying economic development at Harvard and MIT at the time and also looking for the most effective way to give their own money to reduce poverty. They found that cash transfers had a strong evidence base and that the rapid growth of mobile payments technology in emerging markets had opened the door to delivering cash transfers securely and efficiently on an unprecedented scale. They created GiveDirectly as a private giving circle in 2009 and opened it to the public in 2011 after two years of operational testing.*[122]

Next, since she admired their mission, Talia looked at job and volunteer opportunities to see what skills GiveDirectly wanted. They were hiring but did not have local organizations or positions. They were looking for a fundraiser, but Talia is not interested in doing this work for her activism. She signed up for the blog, though. She also decided to direct her charitable contributions to GiveDirectly.

Switching gears, she researched local organizations using the various volunteer databases. She made a list of appealing organizations. These included Junior Achievement, the local animal shelter, a refugee services organization, and an organization helping homeless families.

Research Potential Organizations

The organization that sparked her interest the most was the refugee services because they focus on providing their clients with a thorough introduction to the community, including help with seeking services like financial accounts and loans. Her research showed the other charities had more attention than this one, so she continued her focus on this neglected cause.

Elevator Speech

Talia fine-tuned her elevator speech.

> *I work in financial services and have skills in financial counseling and loan products. My most significant joy comes from helping families improve their financial capability because it impacts so many areas of their lives positively. I want to change the way we welcome immigrants to our country by providing them with tools and help to become capable quickly.*

Activist Interview

Talia interviewed a friend who works for a nonprofit giving emergency help to families in crisis. Although her friend did not do the financial counseling aspect of the work, she was able to answer Talia's questions.

Question: What were experiences essential to your development?

Answer: Not to take the work home with you. To celebrate all accomplishments, no matter how small.

Q: What advice do you have for me?

A: To understand not everyone has the skills and knowledge we have, and many experienced terrible circumstances. Being in a crisis that involves their kids is so difficult for them. Be empathetic.

Q: How did you prepare to work with those who are different from you?

A: I shadowed other volunteers for a month before I started working on my own. This allowed me to get a feel for the clients and ask questions of the other volunteers.

Q: Did you encounter any areas where you were unprepared? How did it inform your activism?

A: I was unprepared for the magnitude of the needs of some families. But that just made me more motivated to volunteer.

Q: Do you have anyone I should talk to?

A: You may want to contact Brad at Family Helpers. He works with non-English-speaking clients.

Ready Yourself

Talia is confident in her ability to do the work. She is motivated about the work itself, its impact, and the way it overlaps with her personal goals. Her inner critic has not been active.

Set Goal for Discussion with Organization

Specific - be very clear about the action you will perform.	Sit down with the director of Refugee Services to find out about opportunities.
Measurable - how will you know you have accomplished it?	I get the information I need from the director.
Achievable - make sure your action can be achieved, is realistic.	Yes. I've done a lot of work on my self-assessment and research.
Relevant - does this action move you forward in your cause?	This is the cause I'm most interested in so I want to make sure it is a fitting match.
Timely – when will you perform this action?	I will schedule it within a week and hope to have the discussion within 2 weeks.

Discussion with a Leader from the Organization

Talia met with Bobbie, the director of Refugee Services. From Bobbie, Talia learned about their history and how they use their resources. Bobbie told Talia that right now they need hands-on workers and interpreters in Spanish and Arabic.

Talia asked questions about how Refugee Services treats its volunteers. It has a volunteer coordinator who tries to match the volunteer with the work they want to do. Bobbie introduced Talia to Julie, who gave more detail about how she manages volunteers. She described a typical day for volunteers, and after Talia pressed, a little bit about issues volunteers face and how she works to avoid them. For example, the work sometimes fluctuates, so there is a tough workload one week but a light workload the next. Julie assured Talia the type of skills she brings are of immense value to the clients. She gave Talia the contact information for one of the volunteers, John, so she could check with him about the work.

Checking in with a Volunteer from the Organization

Talia made an appointment to speak with John over the phone. She described her interest in the organization and why she was calling.

John said he is happy working for Refugee Services. Before he volunteered there, he had been involved in other organizations that didn't seem to care about him as a person and what he wanted to do. He gave props to Julie for trying to make sure the volunteers were fulfilled, although he cautioned that she was not always able to do that completely.

Talia asked how they developed him as an activist. John hadn't thought about that before, but as he mulled it over, he realized when Julie checked in with him, she always asked whether he was feeling positive about what he was doing. He always said yes, but he told Talia he believed Julie would listen to a no answer and help him. He remembers, too, he was singing to himself in the break room and she asked him if he would sing at a fundraiser, which was an experience he really enjoyed.

John recommended the organization to Talia.

Talia's Choice

Talia signed up to volunteer for Refugee Services.

Chapter Summary

All your previous work pays off as you make a final choice and use the tools provided in this chapter to have a discussion with your target organization.

Research the organization for which you want to work. What is its mission statement and is it living up to that mission? What do others say about its impact? A template helps you interview an activist who is working in your cause, so you can gather information about the work and get advice for moving forward.

Finally, using the tools provided, you prepare for and conduct an interview with a leader from your target organization. If the opportunity seems right, follow up with a current volunteer to make sure the organization provides the support you need.

Talia's work to find the best match for working in her cause paid off with her choice of Refugee Services. Because of her dedicated assessment she has a cause she is passionate about and that matches her gifts.

Hopefully, you have navigated your assessment and found an activism opportunity that motivates you, too.

In the next chapter, you will take steps to make sure you perform well in your new opportunity.

Activist in Action: Sparky Rucker

My father, J. D. Rucker, Sr. was a WWII veteran who, along with his brothers who were also vets, were appalled that they returned home from war to a segregated life that afforded more courtesies to ex-Nazi's than to honorable, loyal black vets. They started one of the first civil rights organizations in our hometown of Knoxville, TN. ~ Sparky Rucker

Sparky Rucker and members of the Black Student Union at The University of Tennessee, 1967

Why did you choose your activism cause?

I was born in 1946 right smack dab in the middle of "Jim Crow" [which was in effect from 1866 to well after I graduated college]. I grew up living in the projects [affordable housing that was part of Franklin Roosevelt's Works Progress Administration]. I attended segregated schools and lived in a segregated neighborhood.

One set of projects that I lived in was one street over from Beaumont Avenue, which was the dividing line between the black projects and the white projects…and Beaumont Avenue was the "no man's land" where the neighborhood Mom & Pop stores were, which served both communities. When you went to the store, you'd carry a pocket full of rocks in case you had to fight your way home. No way to live.

My father, J. D. Rucker, Sr. was a WWII veteran who, along with his brothers who were also vets, were appalled that they returned home from war to a segregated life that afforded more courtesies to ex-Nazi's than to honorable, loyal black vets. They started one of the first civil rights organizations in our hometown of Knoxville, Tennessee. The Young Man's Civic League became well known and changed many things in Knoxville. Everyone in the family became members of the N.A.A.C.P., and it started me on the path of social activism.

How did you decide what method to use for your activism?

I don't know how old I was, but I do remember being in one of my first demonstrations. I was with my Mother, Louretta T. Rucker. We were at a "pray in," in front of Rich's Department Store. Rich's, who had its home base in Atlanta, Georgia, was one of the many stores during Jim Crow times that did not allow African Americans to eat at their lunch counters. Since the laws required "special permits" in order for us to have protest marches in my hometown of Knoxville, Tennessee, it was decided that we would all gather in front of the store to "pray," thereby "breaking no laws." My recollection is that I was not sure that I would be "non-violent."

Picture me "praying" with one fist balled up and suspiciously looking around in fear. As I looked down the road, I spied a "dirty-looking street person" who I thought must have been the "worst kind of redneck!" I prepared myself for receiving and giving many kicks and blows. As the man approached, he stared at me and ... then he smiled and said, "howdy!" as he walked on by. It was a lesson learned … and as Bo Diddley says, "You can't judge a book by looking at the cover."

Oh, and the result of our protest? Well, we caused Rich's to lose over one million dollars in revenue and forced it to close its Knoxville branch. Power to the People!

Later I found that my ability to gather people together in song was the way I could best contribute to the cause. I led the singing at many mass meetings and on many picket lines and marches.

What advice do you have for new activists?

Agitate, agitate, AGITATE!!!

Sparky Rucker is a long-time activist and musician. Before he began his full-time music career he was a schoolteacher, and he still educates children through his concerts and recordings. Read more about Sparky and his music at http://www.sparkyandrhonda.com.

PART 5

Your Passion in Action

In Part 5 focus on a solid plan to achieve your activism goals and support your efforts. Because activism is sometimes challenging, check in with your impact and reactions so you can stay motivated. Finally, celebrate your accomplishments.

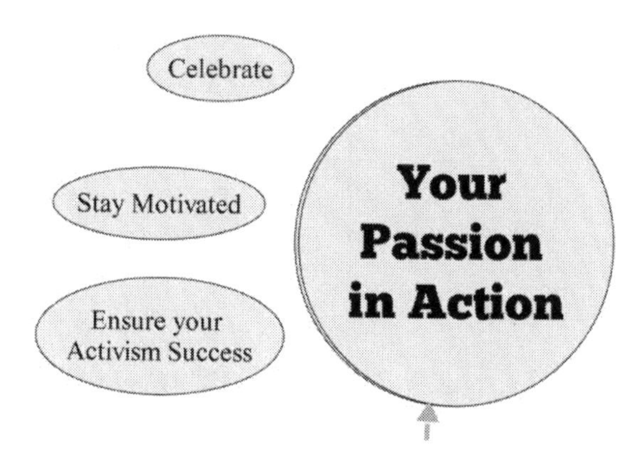

Part 5 includes:

Chapter 11: Ensure Your Activism Success

Chapter 12: Stay Motivated

Chapter 13: Celebrate Your Work

CHAPTER 11

Ensure Your Activism Success

No snowflake in an avalanche ever feels responsible.

~ George Burns [123]

Objective

Plan for maximum activism impact.

Goal

Make a plan to maximize your performance.

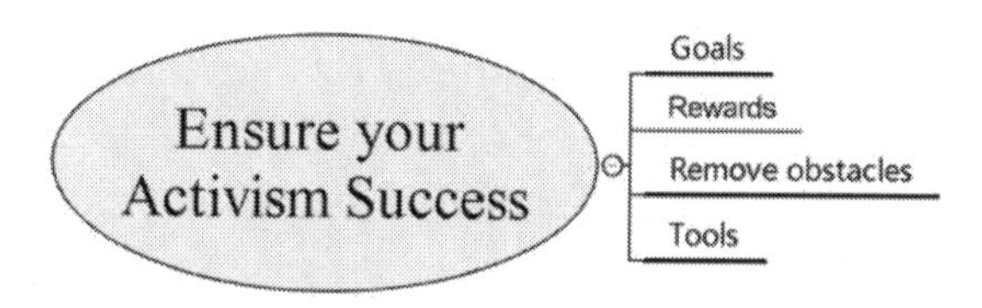

HOPEFULLY, YOU'VE MADE SATISFACTORY progress on examining what you bring to activism. In this chapter, you will explore how rewards, punishments, tools, and obstacles affect your work and how to ensure you are successful.

Your Choice

You've finally chosen the organization and position you wish for your activism.

Congratulations! You've put in hard work to do your homework and make sure you are on the right path to affect your cause. Pat yourself on the back!

Factors impacting performance

You want your work to make a difference, so look at the factors affecting your performance. Psychologist Robert Mager has tips on how to increase the odds of positive results.[124] Understand how your skills and knowledge, motivation (rewards and punishments), and tools and obstacles impact your performance. Finally, locate barriers you can remove and ask for the tools you need.

Skills and Knowledge

In earlier chapters, you named your skills and knowledge for activism work. You may also have identified areas where you need to gain more insight or train for better skills.

Performing a task is not just about having the right skills and knowledge, though. When I try a task, I need skill, knowledge, and motivation for success. But even with those factors, I am not always successful.

For example, I like to try new recipes. I have skill and knowledge. I enjoy cooking and eating the dish. I'm motivated because I enjoy the process of cooking and a delicious meal. What could go wrong? Mixed-up motivation.

Motivation: Rewards and Punishments

As I perform tasks, I want to continue to do the activities that reward me. For example, I like to have a clean desk, so the job of tidying provides me with the reward of serenity.

For another person, tidying a desk may be punishing. Tidying is not fun, and they don't value a clean desk as I do. Doing the task is punishing, and they will tend to avoid it in the future.

Sometimes the rewards and punishments get mixed up and lead people to continue to do punishing tasks or stop doing rewarding tasks. For example, there is that person in the office who always does an excellent job—so much so that her supervisor looks to her more often than others. She gets more work when she does the job right, and her co-workers get less work for doing the job wrong. Mixed-up motivation means doing the job right punishes her.

Suppose I manage to create my new dish, and it's yummy, but I have an allergic reaction to it. Creating the meal was fun but eating the dish is punishing. I will not make the dish again.

In an activism setting, mixed-up motivation might look like this:

- I go to a nonviolent protest, and someone hits me with a rock; I won't go to a protest again.
- I don't gather all the petition signatures assigned to me, and others must gather them for me. I'm rewarded for not doing my job. I'll slack off in the future.

Tools

The right tools make cooking easier. If I am using my oven and the power goes out, the lack of this tool will ruin my dish. Recently I wanted to try a new recipe, but I needed a jackfruit, which I've never heard of or seen in a grocery store. Or a recipe may call for a tool I don't have in my kitchen, like a dish I wanted to make that needed a Spiralizer. Even with the right skills, knowledge, and motivation, the lack of proper tools will hamper performance.

In an activism setting lack of tools might look like this:

~ I don't have the right software to compile a mailing list
~ I have no postage stamps for mailings
~ I need a clear backpack to meet the requirements for entry into a protest area

Obstacles

Obstacles can get in the way in our lives and stop us from doing what we want to do. I head to a meeting, and my car breaks down. I need to take my dog for a walk, but I don't have time. I want to work on task A, but my boss insists on task B.

Removing potential obstacles improves my chances of success. I can't predict my car is going to break down when I head to a meeting, but if I drive an old car, better maintenance and roadside service will help. I want to take my dog for a walk, and he wants it, too. I can schedule time in my planner.

In an activism setting, obstacles may include:

- ~ You are having trouble procuring the right permit for a protest.
- ~ To launch a campaign for city council, a candidate must raise funds. Having the skill, knowledge, and motivation is fantastic, but she will also need funding for success.
- ~ You want to attend a rally, but your partner questions your safety and asks you not to go. This situation needs a conversation with your partner about how you are ensuring your safety and whether that quells his or her fears. Then you can attend the rally without damaging your relationship.

Maximize your performance

You want to make a difference in your work, so maximize your performance. Robert Mager has tips on how to increase the odds of excellent performance; as you mull over your desired activism opportunities, learn to recognize the impact of performance factors.[125] Here is a framework: Start with an activism task.

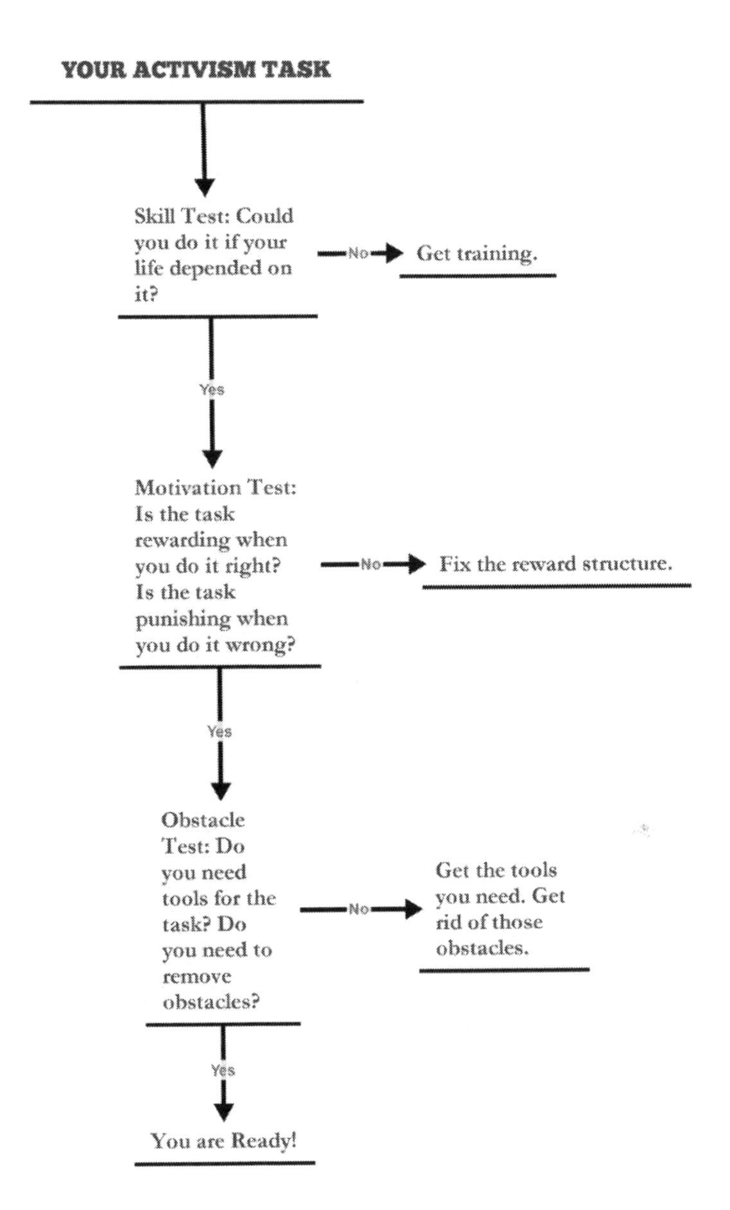
YOUR ACTIVISM TASK
Skill Test: Could you do it if your life depended on it?
No
Get training.
Yes
Motivation Test: Is the task rewarding when you do it right? Is the task punishing when you do it wrong?
No
Fix the reward structure.
Yes
Obstacle Test: Do you need tools for the task? Do you need to remove obstacles?
No
Get the tools you need. Get rid of those obstacles.
Yes
You are Ready!

Question #1, Skill and Knowledge Test. Can you do the task if your life depends on it?

If the answer is "No," then you must pursue training. If the answer is "Yes," but you aren't doing the task, check your motivation. Move to Question #2.

Question #2, Motivation Test. Is the task rewarding when you do it right? Is the task punishing when you do it wrong?

The way rewards and punishments are set up in work can affect your motivation. If you get rewarded for doing it right and punished for doing it wrong, you are strongly motivated. But what if you are penalized for doing it right and rewarded for doing it wrong? Change the rewards or punishments that affect your work to maximize your performance.

If the answer to the question, "Is the task rewarding when you do it right?" is "No," then you must change the reward structure. If the answer to the question, "Is the task punishing when you do it wrong?" is "No," then you must change the punishment structure.

If the answer to both questions is "Yes," but you can't do the task, check for obstacles. Move to Question #3.

Question #3, Obstacle Test. If skill, knowledge, and motivation are not issues but performance is still a problem, can you get tools or remove obstacles?

If the answer is "No," then reconsider performing the task at all. Refocus on a different activism task.

If the answer is "Yes," remove obstacles, get the tools you need, and start!

You have the skill, knowledge, and motivation to start on your cause. If all those factors are in place, success is likely, but let's look at other factors that affect your success.

Identify and remove obstacles: Who stands in the way of you being successful as an activist? Why are they standing in your way and how can you change that? Who stands in the way of you making changes?

Rewards for doing it right: How can you make this experience as reinforcing to you as possible, so you continue to want to do it? Tailor this to your activism choice and what makes you motivated. As you negotiate your terms in the discussion, talk about your motivation and make sure important elements are part of the job. Reward yourself for achieving individual goals intrinsically (a pat-on-the-back reminder that you are fantastic for securing 500 signatures on your petition), or extrinsically (a lovely dessert with a friend at a café).

Punishment for doing it wrong: How can you avoid making this experience punishing? Again, this is personal based on your cause and your own motivations. But as you negotiate your terms, tell them what you want to avoid in your activism work. For example, you are willing to canvass door-to-door when an emergency need arises, but you do not wish to do it as your primary job. Other ideas - activism conflicting with important life events is punishing. Don't miss your kid's games because you signed up as a greeter every Saturday. You'll just end up quitting and that does you and your cause no good.

Jacinda's Story

Jacinda became interested in Bernie Sander's message, and after the election, she volunteered to work for The People's Party. Her motivation for encouraging Sanders to run for a third party was intense. Her skills were analysis, writing, programming, and creativity. Her dislikes were talking on the phone, social interaction, and quick decision-making. She was not well organized.

Her first volunteer task was to get others to sign a petition to be presented to Sanders. Although she knew this was important to the cause, she didn't want to stand up and make a speech, or canvass, because it required social interaction. But she attended several meetings of various coalitions to get signatures.

Her second volunteer job was organizing a watch party for the night the petition was presented to Sanders. This involved organizing, in which she is not skilled, and party planning, which she had never done.

Because she managed to pull off the watch party, the People's Party leader asked her to become the state organizer. She told the leader she did not have this skill set but he pressed her, and because she believed in the cause, she said yes. As a state leader, her job was to recruit volunteers and build coalitions, both tasks she had never done.

It was apparent the technology useful for these tasks was lacking, and she wondered if her skills could help with this. She asked, but they kept her in her current slot.

The organization used phone calls for communication, even though she preferred to use email or chat. Because she worked full time, she would do her volunteer work in the evening, and on the way home, she found herself feeling dread at having to do activities she hated. Stressed and drained, she notified the organization this was not the right volunteer job for her, and now she is not doing much work for the group at all.

Analyzing Jacinda's situation using the framework

Jacinda's Task: State leader for the People's Party.

Question #1, Skill and Knowledge Test: Can you do the task if your life depends on it?

Skills needed: coalition building and recruiting (Jacinda lacked these skills, so no)

Question #2, Motivation Test: Is the task rewarding when you do it right? Is the task punishing when you do it wrong?

Even though Jacinda was strongly motivated for the cause, she had trouble performing the tasks because of her lack of skills. If she managed to complete a task, she received appreciation from the organization leader but also felt a great deal of stress.

Question #3, Obstacle Test: If skill, knowledge, and motivation are not issues but performance is still a problem, can you get tools or remove obstacles?

Jacinda's leader did not respond to her requests and concerns. Jacinda's motivation for the cause was strong, but she was assigned volunteer tasks and a role focused on her weaknesses. The dread and stress (punishments) associated with trying to perform these tasks made the job draining even with the appreciation from the organization leader (reward). Jacinda had strong skills in other areas to help the campaign, and despite asking to switch roles, the leader chose to keep her in her current position because they lacked bench strength. It took a few months, but Jacinda became so fatigued she quit the work.

The volunteer coordinator should have responded to Jacinda's concerns about her ability to do the job. If placing somebody in a role for which they have limited skills is short term, it may work. But over the long run, the organization risks burning out a dedicated volunteer.

Considering skills, motivation, knowledge, tools, and obstacles can lead to a better match for an activist to a job. This framework might have prevented a motivated volunteer from becoming frustrated and uninterested in helping.

Go to Chapter 11 in *The WOYS? Workbook*

Activism Goals

I hope you are celebrating your activism choice and the blessing of having a place to make a difference in the world.

Have a few SMART goals in place as you begin your work. Also, planning will help you stay motivated, assess whether you are making a difference, know when you are feeling stressed and need a break, and what to do about it.

As a reminder, goals and feedback are enormous boosts for performance in any part of your life. As you begin your activism journey, take time to set measurable goals. Then later, you will check back against these goals and hopefully recognize the impact you've had. And reward yourself!

Bridget's Story

Here are Bridget's SMART goals for her first year of activism:

Specific - be very clear about the action you will perform.	Sit down with the director of Refugee Services to find out about opportunities.
Measurable - how will you know you have accomplished it?	I get the information I need from the director.
Achievable - make sure your action can be achieved, is realistic.	Yes. I've done a lot of work on my self-assessment and research.
Relevant - does this action move you forward in your cause?	This is the cause I'm most interested in so I want to make sure it is a fitting match.
Timely – when will you perform this action?	I will schedule it within a week and hope to have the discussion within 2 weeks.

Go to Chapter 11 in *The WOYS? Workbook*

Talia's Story

Talia's main activism goal is to become a financial counselor for female refugees. She uses the framework to maximize her performance.

Question #1, Skill and Knowledge Test: Could you do it if your life depended on it?

The reason this is important and meaningful is if female refugees understand our monetary systems, they can use them to build financial capability. Talia knows she has the right skills and knowledge for this worthy cause.

Question #2, Motivation Test: Is the task rewarding when you do it right? Is the task punishing when you do it wrong?

The task is rewarding when Talia does it right because she wants to see an impact on her activism and she believes this work will make a difference in the women's lives. It will also prepare her for taking on a more significant role in the organization which is part of fulfilling her life plan. Talia does not yet know the impact if she does the task wrong.

Question #3, Obstacle Test: Can you get tools or remove obstacles?

One obstacle she sees is a language barrier with her clients. Although it will not prevent her from doing the work, because there are interpreters, she wants to make a direct connection with her clients.

Talia's goal for the first week of her activism:

Specific - be very clear about the action you will perform.	Understand the financial options available to clients through the program before my orientation.
Measurable - how will you know you have accomplished it?	I will check during my orientation to ensure I understand the options.
Achievable - make sure your action can be achieved, is realistic.	Yes, I can read the manual before my orientation.
Relevant - does this action move you forward in your cause?	Yes. The financial options for clients are a core service I will provide.
Timely – when will you perform this action?	By my orientation on Wednesday.

Her goal for the first month of her activism:

Specific - be very clear about the action you will perform.	Enroll in a course in Arabic so I can better work directly with immigrants from Africa.
Measurable - how will you know you have accomplished it?	Actual enrollment.
Achievable - make sure your action can be achieved, is realistic.	It will take time to find the best place to learn Arabic. One month will be enough.
Relevant - does this action move you forward in your cause?	Yes. Although I am not expecting to become fluent, having a basic foundation of common phrases will help me better connect and serve clients.
Timely – when will you perform this action?	By the end of the month.

Her goal for the first year of her activism:

Specific - be very clear about the action you will perform.	Manage the organization's finances.
Measurable - how will you know you have accomplished it?	They will approve me to perform this job.
Achievable - make sure your action can be achieved, is realistic.	I believe a year is long enough for me to establish my skills, knowledge, and reliability.
Relevant - does this action move you forward in your cause?	Yes. This is the next step in my plan to serve this cause.
Timely – when will you perform this action?	By the end of the year.

Chapter Summary

You have chosen your activism opportunity. Congratulations! Make sure you have the foundation in place for successful performance.

Hopefully, you've made progress examining what you bring to activism. Now explore how rewards, punishments, tools, and obstacles might impact your work and how to ensure you are successful.

Effective performance is a mixture of the right skills, knowledge, motivation, and circumstances. For an activist beginning the work, examining effective performance improves the odds of making a positive impact.

Bridget and Talia set goals and examined what gets in the way of successful performance.

You examined performance factors in this chapter so you can ensure you have the right resources to perform your activism work. If you don't have what you need, pinpoint what needs to change for your effectiveness. This involves being proactive as you work with organizations to ask for what you need.

In the next chapter, you will take steps to stay motivated in your activism. You will check your progress against your goals. You will also take care of yourself

CHAPTER 12

Stay Motivated

Love, once again, break our hearts open wide.

~ Reverend Jason Shelton [126]

Objective

Stay motivated in your activism.

Goal

Check on your progress. Take care of yourself.

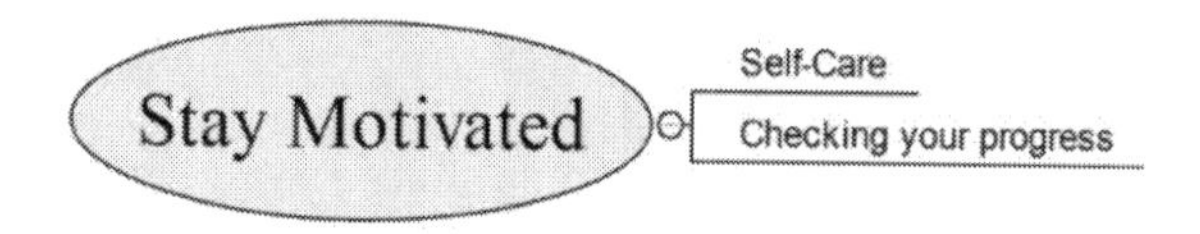

SETTING GOALS WILL IMPROVE YOUR performance, even more so if they are moderately challenging. If you do a great job using the SMART process to establish your goals, you will have a decent idea of how to check whether you are making progress. Your goals are already measurable.

Sometimes you may need to ask others for the feedback you need. In fact, proactively seek input about how you are doing. Supervisors see employees who ask for feedback as more interested and competent.[127] In fact, seeking negative feedback (e.g., what can I do better?) makes people see you as more effective. In a busy activism movement, you may not get feedback on a regular basis, so ask for it.

Seeking feedback will result in improved performance because you get the information you need to review and potentially refocus your goals. Goal adjustment means better performance and, surprisingly, better wellbeing and health.[128]

Asking for feedback is hard but vital to your activism success.

Use the feedback you receive to adjust your goals or set new goals. Legendary women's basketball coach Pat Summitt spent many years at the top of her profession but never stopped setting goals. Years ago, I had the opportunity to hear her speak and asked her a question about goals: Does she focus her team on winning each game, or the SEC tournament, or the National Championship? She responded that she stayed laser-focused on what was happening every minute of every practice. And, to always "continue to seek new goals."

Go to Chapter 12 in *The WOYS? Workbook*

Monica's Story

One year into advocating for people with disabilities, Monica checks her progress. She had set a goal to raise awareness of issues faced by those with disabilities by broadcasting their stories and using public outrage to encourage change.

The results were mixed. Monica was successful at raising awareness of times when people with a disability are mistreated. She started a Facebook page devoted to the stories to reach a broad audience. Every month she highlighted the experience of a person with a disability in her town. By the end of the year, she had featured 12 stories, and three people experienced positive changes. Her Facebook page had 1800 followers.

She was disappointed only three people with disabilities saw change because of the stories. It was a lot of work to interview people, get photos, and write an excellent narrative. She decided to ask a friend with a marketing background for feedback.

Her friend was less critical of Monica's efforts, pointing out she was in the beginning stages of building her follower base. She suggested that Monica also use Twitter to target more young people. But her best idea was to establish a relationship with a newspaper reporter to get the stories featured more broadly. Monica made contact and the reporter got one of the stories published in the paper, resulting in an immediate change for the person with the disability. The reporter also said she would feature Monica's stories in the future.

Reenergized, she set new goals for the next year.

Stay Motivated: Self-Care

Stress Awareness

Reverend Jason Shelton's words, "Love, once again, break our hearts open wide" are the lyrics to a song he wrote after the Charlottesville protests. Love is the root of change, and he recognizes we must keep our hearts open wide.

Activism can bring opportunities for stress. It frustrates me when people don't believe the same way I do and don't respond to my logic. But I can't realize my goals if I get frustrated.

In addition to conflict with others who believe differently, I may stress myself about what actions I take or don't take. My inner critic takes over from my inner mentor.

What stresses you? Your safety may concern you. Or perhaps you are okay about the risks you are taking, but your family is worried.

You may have less time with your family.

Ugliness can permeate your dealings with others, but you've decided the trouble is worth the impact on your cause. You've drawn the line between what you are willing to take versus what you cannot accept.

Now, as you prepare to enter your activism role, recognize what you need to do to take care of yourself on this journey. Your cause is important; ensure your self-care so it receives the benefit of your best work.

When I was in high school, I played the piano for the chorus. If the music needed a long, sustained note, more than one person's breath capacity, the choir took turns leaving the music, taking a breath, and coming back in. This is a lovely way to look at how you can care for yourself and then come back into your work in an energized way.

How do you know when you need to take a breath? This will vary, as everyone experiences stress and fatigue in diverse ways. Change is stressful and entering activism is a change in your life circumstances that needs time for adjustment.

Learn what stress symptoms appear in your body and use this checklist from Baylor University to rate your overall stress level.

Go to Chapter 12 in *The WOYS? Workbook*

Use Coping Strategies

Coping strategies help you head off stress before it becomes overwhelming. Proactive stress reduction means before things get really tough, take action. Solve problems, get help from your support network, and assert your needs.

Use your Support Network

Earlier, you named people who give excellent support to you and added them to your support network. As you reflect on using relationships as a coping strategy, are they the ones to help? Do they make you feel better? Are they honest and guide you in ways to cope and live healthier?

Control Your Reactions

Control your reactions to events by training your mind to interpret them in a more rational, positive way. This may include disputing negative self-talk, making your default reactions positive rather than negative, and using logic rather than emotions.

Self-Management

Use self-management to deal with stress and improve functioning. Keep track of your body's reactions and release pent-up emotions, manage negative feelings, and use systematic relaxation procedures. The methods that work with the most symptoms of stress are progressive relaxation and exercise.[129]

My Buddhist friends note I cause my own anxiety by dwelling on the past or fretting about the future, rather than being present in the moment. Reflect on whether you look backward and dwell on the past and how that can lead to depression. Or whether you look forward and fret, which can lead to excessive anxiety. How much less stress would you have to deal with if you stayed focused on the present?

Incorporate gratefulness into your work

Gratefulness has a positive impact on wellbeing, resilience, and life satisfaction. It also reduces anxiety, stress, and depression. [130] [131] Individuals who each day list five things they are grateful for showed stress reductions over a five-week period.

Gratitude also positively impacts social networks because folks who receive appreciation pay it forward to others. This type of social network can help everyone cope better.[132]

Go to Chapter 12 in *The WOYS? Workbook*

Eric's Story

Erik Marcus found himself in terrible health after spending several decades working in an activism area involving much cruelty. He finally woke up to the physical symptoms and realized he had to make changes. Now he focuses on making sure he does not make activism his complete focus at the expense of a balanced life. He does yoga, listens to the signals his body provides, and handles painful emotions rather than suppressing them.

> *"Done properly, activism can be carried out in a way that promotes self-healing. Whatever direction your advocacy takes, know that it all begins with a commitment to self-love and self-care. If you're gentle with yourself, you'll be gentle on the people you aspire to persuade."* [133]

Do You Need to Change Your Activism Focus?

You may find yourself stressed by your activism to a degree you believe you can't control it with coping strategies. In that case, see whether you need to refocus your activism efforts. As Erik Marcus reminds us, advocacy needs to start with self-love and self-care.

If, despite using coping strategies, you cannot manage your stress, look for opportunities to step back. Remind yourself your health means you have more chance to make an impact and taking a break is okay.

Take time off and come back refreshed.

If it doesn't help, consider negotiating a different role in the same organization. Make sure this role gives you the same joy and impact as your earlier one.

Change Focus if Necessary

If the need to choose a different focus altogether arises, go back to the assessment work you've done and see what other direction your passion takes you. Work the process so you are still using your skills and knowledge, are motivated, and are making the change you want in the world.

Go to Chapter 12 in *The WOYS? Workbook*

Megan's Story

Megan was spending about 20 hours a week advocating for a living wage. She loved using her corporate experience to better understand how to lobby business leaders for the living wage. Because of her efforts, she got one organization to raise its pay structure.

Unfortunately, she was diagnosed with breast cancer, and health concerns prevented her from continuing her activism work. She had to take time to care for herself and get well. She had no family history of breast cancer and lived a healthy lifestyle. While researching her disease, she uncovered many studies showing the potential impact of toxins in products such as lotions, shampoos, and cosmetics. Formaldehyde, for instance, which is commonly used as a preservative in cosmetics, is linked to cancer. Coal tar, which is used as a colorant and an anti-dandruff agent, is a known carcinogen.[134]

Megan was horrified to discover her exposure. Did the toxins cause or contribute to her cancer? As she continued her treatment and eventually achieved remission, she educated herself about the issue of toxins in household products. Hugely motivated to make change in this area, she refocused her activism and is using her business and activism experience to lobby for clean, toxin-free products.

Talia's Story

Staying Motivated: Check your progress

Talia set goals for the first week, month, and year of her activism. They are measurable. She also sees Julie as a potential source of feedback.

Staying Motivated: Self-care

Recognizing stress

Talia worked with a refugee named Benedicta. She had to flee her birthplace in the Congo and move to Kenya. Her family forced her to marry young. This was difficult for Talia to hear and she recognized her reactions reflected in her body. When stressed, Talia stiffens her shoulders, clenches her jaw, and gets teary, which she did in hearing

Benedicta's story. Afterward, she spoke with Julie and felt reassured her response was genuine and appreciated by Benedicta, but Julie recommended relaxation techniques.

Coping Strategies

Talia has an active meditation practice, although she's not always skilled at staying in the present moment. She tends to look forward and fret about what might happen. She keeps, sporadically, a daily gratitude journal.

She has started to put exercise as a priority, to reduce stress.

She realized not getting her needs met may lead to burnout and a reduced ability to help her clients. She will watch herself for potential impacts of stress: not being able to do the job as well, not being able to think as well, exhaustion, PTSD, and physical problems.

Elements of self-care she included were checking in with her body during meditation, throughout the day, and in stressful situations. This may result in having to change her self-talk, exercising to release painful emotions, and becoming more assertive about what she needs.

She mulled over checking in more with her support network.

Change focus if necessary

At this point, Talia is not considering a change of activism focus. She is still motivated and believes she can manage the stress. She takes great pleasure in her work and feels grateful she can make a difference in the lives of these people.

Chapter Summary

Now that you have embarked on your plans for change, make sure you build in steps to ensure you stay motivated and continue to make an impact. You will do this by setting goals that keep you motivated. As you do your activism work, you will monitor your stress levels, use coping skills, and change your focus if necessary.

Megan used her skills in one way until illness forced her to reevaluate her options. Talia used the process to ensure she is still motivated and healthy.

Do you know what to do to stay motivated in your activism work? Check your progress and take care of yourself.

In the final chapter, you will honor the work you have done and celebrate.

Activist in Action: Jenny Arthur

Even if you do not have a lot of money or a big group of people, if there is a truth that needs to be told, go ahead and be that voice. Even if you do not see results, it is a sign of hope, and that has spiritual significance. ~ Jenny Arthur

Why did you choose your activism cause?

Because death does not impact families very often, most people are unprepared when it does. In the midst of grief, they must navigate the sales tactics of the funeral industry, and many end up purchasing services that they do not want, at great expense. This is a great burden on the poor, especially. People take on huge debts, and sometimes abandon the bodies of loved ones at the morgue because they cannot afford to claim them. We recently helped a young man save $3000 on his mother's unexpected funeral just by letting him know it was legal to buy her casket online at much less expense.

How did you decide what method to use for your activism?

We started having Death Cafes in Knoxville to create a space for people to talk about death and dying before it happens. Having these conversations helps people be more prepared when it does. I also started Facebook pages for Death Cafe Knoxville and for Funeral Consumers Alliance of East Tennessee. Using social media is the best way to get the message out for us.

Were there areas where you felt unprepared for your work?

The funeral industry has a big, well-funded lobby, and they are continually advocating for laws that would force people to buy goods and services at higher cost, or to take away our right to a home funeral. As a volunteer, it is difficult to keep up.

What advice do you have for new activists?

Even if you do not have a lot of money or a big group of people, if there is a truth that needs to be told, go ahead and be that voice. Even if you do not see results, it is a sign of hope, and that has spiritual significance.

Reverend Jenny Arthur is a Community Minister and runs Borderland Tees, a social enterprise that produces screen-printed t-shirts for businesses, churches, and community organizations, in support of those who are marginalized by mental illness, prison records, and other social factors. She is a graduate of Yale Divinity School and President of Funeral Consumers Alliance of East Tennessee.

CHAPTER 13

Celebrate Your Work

Be a lamp,
a lifeboat,
a ladder. Help someone's soul heal. Walk
out of your
house
like a
shepherd. ~ Rumi

Objective

Recognize yourself for the work you have done to make the change you want in the world.

Goal

Celebrate the work you have done to prepare to make the change you want in the world.

I HOPE MY BOOK HAS HELPED YOU get ready for the change you want to make in the world. After your hard work and self-reflection, I hope you were able to:

~ Identify your activism passions from your consideration of what makes you angry or sad, and what you love and want to protect.
~ Identify the skills you have for making change.
~ Inventory the knowledge you bring to activism.

- Be clear about your personal motivations, and motivation for activism.
- Make an impact, get energized, use your skills, knowledge, and motivation, and grow as an activist.
- Plan for starting in the work, staying motivated, and checking in to make sure you are on the right track.
- Create your protest sign.

I hope my recommendations and tools helped you carry out these tasks.

Go to Chapter 13 in *The WOYS? Workbook*

As you move forward to take your place in making change, I want to give you my sincere thanks. Thank you for caring, whatever your cause. Thank you for acting, on whatever you do. Thank you for taking the risk, at whatever level you choose. Thank you for taking the time, in your life of competing pressures. Thank you for inspiring others, in whatever way it happens. You teach me and others with your work. I feel joyous.

About the Author

Photo by Mark Empey Photography

Terri L. Lyon has a Ph.D. in Industrial and Organizational Psychology from The University of Tennessee, Knoxville. A licensed Psychologist, her career experience includes government, Fortune 500 manufacturing, and education.

Her activism focus is primarily on animals and the environment. Factory farming of animals is terrible in so many ways, and by encouraging plant-based diets, she hopes to end animal cruelty and create a healthier Earth.

Terri is also a consumer activist. She is treasurer of a federal credit union, where members can get financial services without having to support shareholders. She also supports dispute resolution as a professional arbitrator for the Better Business Bureau.

Her family includes her husband, two sons, and many rescue animals. They live in the foothills of the Great Smoky Mountains National Park.

Photo by Mark Empey Photography

To learn more about Terri and to find more resources on activism:

~ The What's On Your Sign? website:
https://WhatsOnYourSign.com

~ Read Terri's blog:
https://LifeAtTheIntersection.com

~ Follow Terri on Twitter @LifeAtTheIntSec

~ Like Terri's Facebook Page:
https://www.facebook.com/LifeAtTheIntSec/

Acknowledgments

When I couldn't find the resources I wanted to get started in activism, I knew there many people like me that were in the same situation. Since I had spent a multitude of hours researching and putting together the processes I decided to write it down so others could find their passion for activism.

November is NaNoWriMo – National Novel Writing Month. I decided I would spend November putting the material together. At the end of November, I had a draft! I appreciate the support of the NaNoWriMo community who make it seem possible to write a book. This book is proof that it is.

My fantastic editor Trish Richert contributed to this book in many ways. After she reviewed my NaNoWriMo draft, she had excellent ideas for the structure of the content. She also suggested creative additions such as interviewing local activists. That's my favorite part of the book now. She walks that tightrope between inspiration and critique perfectly.

Some authors have teams that support them. Trish was that team for me, giving me a push when I needed it. And helping when I asked, even if it wasn't something in her job description. I'm not sure I would have made it without you, Trish!

Cathy Denton, Bill Grant, and Jill England read earlier versions of the book, providing feedback to make it better. Thank you for taking the time to read my manuscript and give me thoughtful feedback.

Hearing the stories of the activists featured in the book was quite inspiring. Thank you to Sue Klaus, Rhonda and Sparky Rucker, Carl Gombert, Nathan Higdon, Summer Awad, and Jenny Arthur. The range of gifts and passions they possess shows me we can find the perfect match and make the change we want to see in the world.

Also Available

Thank you for reading my book!

As a new author, I'm still building my community of readers. Please add a short review on Amazon and let others know how the book can help them get started in activism.

If you are interested in *The What's on Your Sign Workbook*, you can sign up to receive the first three chapters at https://WhatsOnYourSign.com.

NOTES

Chapter 1

[1] Parton, Dolly. (2015, February 27). Quote. Retrieved from https://twitter.com/dollyparton/status/571415379190226944?lang=en

[2] Rettig, H. (2006). *The Lifelong Activist: How to change the world without losing your way*. New York, NY: Lantern Books, p. 267

[3] Nilsson, J. E., Marszalek, J. M., Linnemeyer, R. M., Bahner, A. D., & Misialek, L. H. (2011). Development and Assessment of the Social Issues Advocacy Scale. *Educational and Psychological Measurement, 71*(1), 258–275. https://doi.org/10.1177/0013164410391581

[4] Grohol, J. M. (2016). Grief & Loss After the Election. Retrieved April 4, 2018, from https://psychcentral.com/blog/grief-loss-after-the-election/

[5] Nast, W. M. O. and C. (2018). *Together We Rise Behind the Scenes at the Protest Heard Around the World*. Dey Street Books, p. 264.

[6] About Us – Gamaliel Network. (n.d.). Retrieved April 4, 2018, from http://gamaliel.org/about-us/

[7] James, N. & McCallion, G. (2013). *School Resource Officers: Law Enforcement Officers in Schools.* Congressional Research Service. Retrieved from https://fas.org/sgp/crs/misc/R43126.pdf

[8] Wolf, C.R. (2018). Preventing School Shootings Requires Additional Measures: Early identification and intervention is needed alongside active shooter drills. *Psychology Today*. Retrieved from https://www.psychologytoday.com/us/blog/the-desk-the-mental-

health-lawyer/201806

Chapter 2

[9] Palmer, P. (2000). *Let your life speak*. San Francisco, CA: Jossey-Bass, p. 3.

[10] Capacchione, L. (2001). *Visioning: Ten steps to designing the life of your dreams*. London: Thorsons.

[11] Malycha, C. P., & Maier, G. W. (2017). The Random-Map Technique: Enhancing Mind-Mapping with a Conceptual Combination Technique to Foster Creative Potential. Creativity Research Journal, 29(2), 114–124. https://doi.org/10.1080/10400419.2017.1302763

[12] Zampetakis, L. A., Tsironis, L., & Moustakis, V. (2007). Creativity development in engineering education: the case of mind mapping. Journal of Management Development, 26(4), 370–380. https://doi.org/10.1108/02621710710740110

[13] Peterson, C. (2011). Bucket Lists and Positive Psychology. Retrieved from https://www.psychologytoday.com/us/blog/the-good-life/201102/bucket-lists-and-positive-psychology, par. 6.

[14] Mohr, T. (2014). *Playing Big*. New York, NY: Gotham Books, p. 201.

[15] Mohr, T. (2014). *Playing Big*. New York, NY: Gotham Books, p. 208-209.

[16] Palmer, P. (2000). *Let your life speak*. San Francisco, CA: Jossey-Bass.

[17] Burkholder, R. (2015). *The Activist's Toolkit: Advice and encouragement from an experienced activist to help you be a successful leader in your community*. Portland, Oregon: Rex Burkholder, p. 14.

Chapter 3

[18] Barber, W. and Wilson-Hartgrove, J. (2016). *The Third Reconstruction: Moral Mondays, Fusion Politics, and the Rise of a New Justice Movement*. Boston: Beacon Press.

[19] Engler, P., & Lasoff, S. (2017). *Resistance Guide: how to sustain*

the movement to win.

[20] Joy, M. (2008). *Strategic Action for Animals: A Handbook on Strategic Movement Building, Organizing, and Activism for Animal Liberation*. Melanie Joy.

[21] Sibilla, N. (n.d.). Tennessee Has Fined Residents Nearly $100,000, Just for Braiding Hair. *Forbes*. Retrieved from https://www.forbes.com/sites/instituteforjustice/2018/03/13/tennessee-has-fined-residents-nearly-100000-just-for-braiding-hair/2/#6cb1195f5a6d

[22] Bolles, R. (2017). *What color is your parachute? 2017*. Berkeley, CA: Ten Speed Press.

[23] Rettig, H. (2006). *The Lifelong Activist: How to change the world without losing your way*. New York, NY: Lantern Books, p. 7.

Chapter 4

[24] Baldwin, James. Quote retrieved from https://en.wikiquote.org/wiki/James_Baldwin

[25] Shibata, A. (2007). Exploring intercultural communication issues in online classes. *Explorations in Media Ecology*, 139–148. Shibata discusses Hofstede's work and its application to online learning.

[26] Ce4less.com. (2017). *Core Counselor Competencies: Improving Cultural Competence*. Retrieved from ce4less.com, p. 35-36.

[27] Miami University Women's Center. (n.d.). *Guide to Activism at Miami University*. Retrieved from https://miamioh.edu/student-life/_files/documents/womens-center/wmc-activist-guide.docx, p. 8-9.

[28] Rudolph, D. (n.d.). "White Privilege and Male Privilege" and "Some Notes for Facilitators". Retrieved June 1, 2018, from https://nationalseedproject.org/white-privilege-and-male-privilege

[29] Daring Discussions. (2017). Retrieved from http://daringdiscussions.com, p. 1

[30] Building the World We Dream About: A Welcoming Congregation Curriculum on Race and Ethnicity. (2016, May 25).

Retrieved from https://www.uua.org/racial-justice/curricula/building-the-world-we-dream-about

[31] Killerman, S. (n.d.). Learn about Gender, Sexuality, & Social Justice. Retrieved from http://itspronouncedmetrosexual.com. Reprinted with permission.

[32] This exercise is from the Unitarian Universalist (UUA) Tapestry of Faith Curriculum *Building a World We Dream About.*

[33] Burkholder, R. (2015). *The Activist's Toolkit: Advice and encouragement from an experienced activist to help you be a successful leader in your community*. Portland, Oregon: Rex Burkholder.

[34] Ce4less.com. (2017). *Core Counselor Competencies: Improving Cultural Competence*. Retrieved from ce4less.com.

[35] Jha, R., & Wesely, T. (n.d.). How Privileged Are You? Retrieved from https://www.buzzfeed.com/regajha/how-privileged-are-you?utm_term=.fm7jLoNQp#.caJ8g93W1

[36] Anti-Defamation League. (2007). Personal Self-Assessment of Anti-Bias Behavior. Retrieved from https://www.adl.org/sites/default/files/documents/assets/pdf/education-outreach/

Chapter 5

[37] Moreno, Rita, Quote retrieved from https://www.brainyquote.com/quotes/rita_moreno_855113

[38] Land, S. (2009). *The Idealist.org Handbook to Building a Better World*. New York, NY: The Penguin Group.)

[39] Vrablikova, K., & Zmerli, S. (2017). The Psychology of Political Participation and Social Movement Activism: An Embedded Perspective. In *European Consortium for Political Research*. Prague. Retrieved from https://ecpr.eu/Events/SectionDetails.aspx?SectionID=587&EventID=95

[40] Clary, E. G., Snyder, M., Ridge, R. D., Copeland, J., Stukas, A. A., Haugen, J., & Miene, P. (1998). Understanding and assessing the

motivations of volunteers: A functional approach. *Journal of Personality and Social Psychology, 74*(6), 1516–1530. https://doi.org/10.1037/0022-3514.74.6.1516

[41] Pinder, C. C. (2007). Expectancy Theory of Work Motivation. In *Encyclopedia of Industrial and Organizational Psychology*, pp. 235–238. Thousand Oaks, CA: SAGE Publications, Inc. https://doi.org/10.4135/9781412952651.n91

[42] Seifi, F. (1999). *Three essays on the determinants of economic growth*. University of Ottawa.

Ishida, R., & Okada, M. (2006). Effects of a firm purpose in life on anxiety and sympathetic nervous activity caused by emotional stress: Assessment by psycho-physiological method. *Stress and Health, 22*(4), 275–281. https://doi.org/10.1002/smi.1095

Khutkyy, D. (2014). Proactive Orientation and Individual Activism As Causes of Personal Achievement and Subjective Well-Being. National Research University Higher School of Economics. p. 1–25.

Stukas, A. A., Hoye, R., Nicholson, M., Brown, K. M., & Aisbett, L. (2016). Motivations to Volunteer and Their Associations With Volunteers' Well-Being. *Nonprofit and Voluntary Sector Quarterly, 45*(1), 112–132. https://doi.org/10.1177/0899764014561122

[43] Seifi, F. (1999). *Three essays on the determinants of economic growth*. University of Ottawa.

[44] Piliavin, J. A., & Charng, H.-W. (1990). Altruism: A review of recent theory and research. *Annual Review of Sociology, 16*, 27–65.

Gladwell, M. (2017, June 19). Small Change. Retrieved from https://www.newyorker.com/magazine/2010/10/04/small-change-malcolm-gladwell

[45] Hirsch, E. (2017, June 29). The Problem with Participatory Democracy is the Participants. Retrieved from https://www.nytimes.com/2017/06/29/opinion/sunday/the-problem-with-participatory-democracy-is-the-participants.html

[46] Amnesty International. (2017). Deadly but Preventable

Attacks: Killings and enforced disappearances of those who defend human rights.

[47] Pat Summitt quote from is from https://www.entrepreneur.com/article/278277

Chapter 6

[48] Obama, B. (2008 February 5). Barack Obama's Feb.5 Speech. *The New York Times*. Retrieved from https://www.nytimes.com/2008/02/05/us/politics/05text-obama.html

[49] Rettig, H. (2006). *The Lifelong Activist: How to change the world without losing your way*. New York, NY: Lantern Books, p. 25.

[50] Iser, L. (n.d.). About Lynne. Retrieved from http://www.elder-activists.org/about-lynne.html

[51] Amin T., & Bartlett R., Hammamy R., Rasor P., Sewell M., et al. (Winter 2017). Do you have to be an activist to be a Unitarian Universalist? *UU World*, p. 37.

[52] Han, Hahrie. How Organizations Develop Activists: Civic Associations and Leadership in the 21st Century. Oxford University Press. Kindle Edition.

[53] Clary, E. G., Snyder, M., Ridge, R. D., Copeland, J., Stukas, A. A., Haugen, J., & Miene, P. (1998). Understanding and assessing the motivations of volunteers: A functional approach. *Journal of Personality and Social Psychology, 74*(6), 1516–1530. https://doi.org/10.1037/0022-3514.74.6.1516

Joey. (2017). Talent gaps from the perspective of a talent limited organization. - Effective Altruism Forum. Retrieved November 3, 2017, from http://effective-altruism.com/ea/1gh/talent_gaps_from_the_perspective_of_a_talent/

[54] Han, Hahrie. *How Organizations Develop Activists: Civic Associations and Leadership in the 21st Century*. Oxford University Press. Kindle Edition, p. 17.

[55] CPS Human Resource Services. (2017). The RJP Tool Kit: A

How-To Guide for Developing a Realistic Job Preview. Retrieved from http://www.cpshr.us/workforceplanning/documents/ToolKitRJP.pdf

Earnest, D., Allen, D., & Landis, R. (2011). Mechanisms linking realistic job previews with turnover: A meta-analytic path analysis. *Personnel Psychology*, 865–897. Retrieved from http://onlinelibrary.wiley.com/doi/10.1111/j.1744-6570.2011.01230.x/full

[56] Lauver, K. J., & Kristof-Brown, A. (2001). Distinguishing between Employees' Perceptions of Person–Job and Person–Organization Fit. *Journal of Vocational Behavior, 59*(3), 454–470. https://doi.org/10.1006/jvbe.2001.1807

[57] Usadolo, Q. E. (2016). *The impact of social exchange on volunteer's workplace outcomes in non-profit organisations*. Southern Cross University.

[58] Boezeman, E. J., & Ellemers, N. (2008). Volunteer recruitment: The role of organizational support and anticipated respect in non-volunteer's attraction to charitable volunteer organizations. *Journal of Applied Psychology, 93*(5), 1013–1026. https://doi.org/10.1037/0021-9010.93.5.1013

[59] Han, Hahrie. *How Organizations Develop Activists: Civic Associations and Leadership in the 21st Century*. Oxford University Press. Kindle Edition.

Chapter 7

[60] King, M. (1968) Excerpted from "The Drum Major Instinct", a sermon by Rev. Martin Luther King, Jr. Retrieved from http://www.thekingcenter.org/get-involved

[61] Tackett, Michael. (December 4, 2017). Women Line Up to Run for Office, Harnessing Their Outrage at Trump. *The New York Times*. Retrieved from https://www.nytimes.com/2017/12/04/us/politics/women-candidates-office.html?smid=tw-share&_r=0

[62] Hilstrom, C. (2017). The Trump Effect, One Year Later:

Thousands of Women Running for Office. Retrieved November 10, 2017, from http://www.yesmagazine.org/issues/solidarity/the-trump-effect-one-year-later-thousands-of-women-running-for-office-20171106

[63] Tackett, Michael. (December 4, 2017). Women Line Up to Run for Office, Harnessing Their Outrage at Trump. *The New York Times*. Retrieved from https://www.nytimes.com/2017/12/04/us/politics/women-candidates-office.html?smid=tw-share&_r=0

[64] Congressional Management Foundation. (2011). *Communicating with Congress: Perceptions of Citizen Advocacy on Capitol Hill*. Retrieved from http://www.congressfoundation.org/storage/documents/CMF_Pubs/cwc-perceptions-of-citizen-advocacy.pdf

[65] Feinberg, M., & Willer, R. (2015). From Gulf to Bridge. *Personality and Social Psychology Bulletin, 41*(12), 1665–1681. https://doi.org/10.1177/0146167215607842

[66] Feinberg, M., & Willer, R. (2015). From Gulf to Bridge. *Personality and Social Psychology Bulletin, 41*(12), 1665–1681. https://doi.org/10.1177/0146167215607842

[67] McArdle, E. (August 11, 2017). UUs fight ACA repeal with civil disobedience. *UU World*. Retrieved from https://www.uuworld.org/articles/uus-fight-aca-repeal

[68] Todd, B. & Duda, R. (March 31, 2018). Why operations management is one of the biggest bottlenecks in effective altruism. Retrieved from https://80000hours.org/articles/operations-management/

[69] Learn more about SameSide at https://onsameside.com/.

[70] Rear, J. (March 13, 2018). The results of Veganuary show why the dietary trend is so popular. Verdict. Retrieved from https://www.verdict.co.uk/vegan-facts-results-veganuary-show-dietary-trend-popular/

[71] Prosperity Now. (n.d.). Retrieved from

https://prosperitynow.org/

[72] Quigley, W. (Fall, 2007). Letter to law student interested in social justice. *DePaul Journal for Social Justice*, Vol. *1*(1). Retrieved from https://law.duke.edu/curriculum/pdf/interested_social_justice.pdf

[73] Butler, K. (2017). Inside the Bold New Animal Liberation Movement: No Masks, No Regrets, All the Risk. *Mother Jones*. Retrieved from http://www.motherjones.com/food/2017/11/inside-the-bold-new-animal-liberation-movement-no-masks-no-regrets-all-the-risk/

[74] Amin T., & Bartlett R., Hammamy R., Rasor P., Sewell M., et al. (Winter 2017). Do you have to be an activist to be a Unitarian Universalist? *UU World*, (p. 33).

[75] Goodling, L. B. (2015). *Civic Engagement 2.0: A Blended Pedagogy of Multiliteracies and Activism*. Retrieved from http://scholarworks.gsu.edu/cgi/viewcontent.cgi?article=1160&context=english_diss

[76] Pickert, K. (2014). Tank Man at 25: Behind the Iconic Tiananmen Square Photo. Time Magazine. Retrieved from http://time.com/3809688/tank-man-iconic-tiananmen-photo/

[77] Greer, B. (2008). *Knitting for Good*. Boston, MA: Trumpeter, p. 8.

[78] Quote from Sarah Corbett part of this *The Guardian* article: https://www.theguardian.com/fashion/shortcuts/2017/sep/18/why-craftivists-are-hiding-notes-in-pockets-during-london-fashion-week.

[79] Barrett, D. & Leddy, S. (2008). Assessing Creative Media's Social Impact. The Fledgling Fund. http://www.thefledglinggfund.org/resources/impact

[80] Finneran, P. (2015). *Documentary Impact: Social Change Through Storytelling*, 1–28.

[81] Goodling, L. B. (2015). *Civic Engagement 2.0: A Blended Pedagogy of Multiliteracies and Activism*. Retrieved from http://scholarworks.gsu.edu/cgi/viewcontent.cgi?article=1160&context=english_diss

---

[82] The Diggers Archive. (n.d.). Overview: who were (are) the Diggers? Retrieved from http://www.diggers.org/overview.htm

[83] The Diggers Archive. (n.d.). Video clip from Tribute to the Summer of Love (2017). Retrieved from http://www.diggers.org/revelations_video.htm

[84] V20: Rise, Resist, Unite (n.d.). Retrieved from https://www.vday.org

[85] Lee, S.-J. (2017). Trans Youth Use Theater to Raise Awareness and Change Policy. *Yes! Magazine*. Retrieved from http://www.yesmagazine.org/peace-justice/trans-youth-use-theater-to-raise-awareness-and-change-policy-20171106

[86] Mohammed-akinyela, I. J. (2012). *Conscious Rap Music : Movement Music Revisited: A Qualitative Study*. Georgia State University.

[87] Gladwell, M. (2017, June 19). Small Change. Retrieved from https://www.newyorker.com/magazine/2010/10/04/small-change-malcolm-gladwell

[88] Lee, Y. H., & Hsieh, G. (2013). Does slacktivism hurt activism? The effects of moral balancing and consistency in online activism. *CHI '13 Proceedings of the SIGCHI Conference on Human Factors in Computing Systems*, 811–820. https://doi.org/10.1145/2470654.2470770

[89] Goodling, L. B. (2015). *Civic Engagement 2.0: A Blended Pedagogy of Multiliteracies and Activism*. Retrieved from http://scholarworks.gsu.edu/cgi/viewcontent.cgi?article=1160&context=english_diss

[90] Goodling, L. B. (2015). *Civic Engagement 2.0: A Blended Pedagogy of Multiliteracies and Activism*. Retrieved from http://scholarworks.gsu.edu/cgi/viewcontent.cgi?article=1160&context=english_diss

[91] Edwards, F., Howard, P., & Joyce, M. (2013). *Digital Activism & Non-Violent Conflict*. The authors found no distinct digital device that works across a variety of campaigns, highlights a few research needs: mobile phone use vs. SMS, and mechanics of government-

focused campaigns vs. other-focused ones.

[92] Goodling, L. B. (2015). *Civic Engagement 2.0: A Blended Pedagogy of Multiliteracies and Activism*. Retrieved from http://scholarworks.gsu.edu/cgi/viewcontent.cgi?article=1160&context=english_diss

[93] Goodling, L. B. (2015). *Civic Engagement 2.0: A Blended Pedagogy of Multiliteracies and Activism*. Retrieved from http://scholarworks.gsu.edu/cgi/viewcontent.cgi?article=1160&context=english_diss, p.70-71.

[94] World@nimal.net. (n.d.). Major tactics sit-ins, freedom riders, demonstrations and marches. Retrieved from http://worldanimal.net/social-movements para. 16.

[95] Wood, J. (n.d.). Protests with Lots of People, One Message Most Likely to Sway Politicians. Retrieved April 4, 2018, from https://psychcentral.com/news/2017/04/01/protests-with-lots-of-people-one-message-most-likely-to-sway-politicians/118480.html

[96] Resistance Guide: How to sustain the movement to win. (n.d.). Chapter 2: How do movements work? Retrieved from https://www.guidingtheresistance.org/chapter_two Specifically, "A study by Daniel Gillion at the University of Pennsylvania analyzed civil rights legislation from the 1960s through the 1990s and found that every 10 protests in a representative's district made that representative one percent more likely to vote in favor of civil rights issues--a minor but nonetheless demonstrable effect on legislative progress."

[97] Hond, F., & Bakker, F. (2007). Ideologically Motivated Activism: How Activist Groups Influence Corporate Social Change Activities. *Academy of Management Review, 32*(3), 901–924. https://doi.org/10.5465/AMR.2007.25275682

[98] Fahri, P. (2017). The mysterious group that's picking Breitbart apart, one tweet at a time. *Washington Post*. Retrieved from https://www.washingtonpost.com/lifestyle/style/the-mysterious-group-thats-picking-breitbart-apart-one-tweet-at-a-time/2017/09/22/df1ee0c0-9d5c-11e7-9083-

fbfddf6804c2_story.html?utm_term=.162216b96e29

[99] Goranova, M., & Ryan, L. V. (2014). *Shareholder Activism: A Multidisciplinary Review. Journal of Management* (Vol. 40). https://doi.org/10.1177/0149206313515519

[100] Reed, A. (February 2017). When Do Consumer Boycotts Work? - Room for Debate. Retrieved from https://www.nytimes.com/roomfordebate/2017/02/07/when-do-consumer-boycotts-work par. 9.

[101] Lee, B., Madsen, P., & King, B. (2007). A Political Mediation Model of Corporate Response to Social Movement Activism. *Administrative Science Quarterly*.

[102] Ethical Consumer. (n.d.). Retrieved from http://www.ethicalconsumer.org/

[103] Change.org. (n.d.). Retrieved from https://www.change.org/

Chapter 8

[104] Dass, Ram. Quote retrieved from https://quotefancy.com/quote/897241/Ram-Dass-Each-of-us-finds-his-unique-vehicle-for-sharing-with-others-his-bit-of-wisdom

[105] Bolles, R. (2017). *What color is your parachute? 2017.* Berkeley, CA: Ten Speed Press.

Chapter 9

[106] MacAskill, W. (2016). *Doing Good Better: How Effective Altruism Can Help You Help Others, Do Work that Matters, and Make Smarter Choices About Giving Back*. New York: Avery.

[107] Milton Friedman quote is from the American Enterprise Institute at http://www.aei.org/publication/ten-classic-milton-friedman-quotes/

[108] MacAskill, W. (2016). *Doing Good Better: How Effective Altruism Can Help You Help Others, Do Work that Matters, and Make Smarter Choices About Giving Back*, New York: Avery, p. 181.

[109] Adapted from the MacAskill (2016) criteria for effective

altruism in MacAskill, W. (2016). *Doing Good Better: How Effective Altruism Can Help You Help Others, Do Work that Matters, and Make Smarter Choices about Giving Back*. New York: Avery.

[110] MacAskill, W. (2016). *Doing Good Better: How Effective Altruism Can Help You Help Others, Do Work that Matters, and Make Smarter Choices about Giving Back*, New York: Avery, pp. 185-195.

Chapter 10

[111] Ghandi, Mahatma. This is an interesting story by Lolly Daskall about the quotation. The Story Behind: You Must Be the Change You Wish To See In The World Retrieved from https://www.linkedin.com/pulse/20140813120052-14431679-the-story-behind-you-must-be-the-change-you-wish-to-see-in-the-world/

[112] Regan, B. (2017). Warning: This Job is Not Perfect (Realistic Job Previews Can Help). Retrieved June 9, 2018, from http://www.selectinternational.com/blog/warning-this-job-is-not-perfect-realistic-job-previews-can-help, par. 4.

[113] Daylight, T. B. (2017). "The difficulty is the point": teaching spoon-fed students how to really read | Books | *The Guardian*. Retrieved June 9, 2018, from https://www.theguardian.com/books/2017/dec/24/the-difficulty-is-the-point-teaching-spoon-fed-students-how-to-really-read, par. 36.

[114] Cruz, M. K. (2016). Watchworthy Wednesday: Check Facts with Crap Detection Resources - DML Central. Retrieved June 9, 2018, from https://dmlcentral.net/watchworthy-wednesday-check-facts-crap-detection-resources/

[115] Burkholder, R. (2015). *The Activist's Toolkit: Advice and encouragement from an experienced activist to help you be a successful leader in your community*. Portland, Oregon: Rex Burkholder.

[116] Kamou, 2014. Effects of shadowing and supervised on-the-job inductions on mental health nurses. *Journal of Psychiatric and Mental Health Nursing*, Vol *21*(4).

[117] Sonnenberg, M., Zijderveld, V. Van, & Brinks, M. (2014).

The role of talent-perception incongruence in effective talent management. Journal of World Business, 49, 272–280. https://doi.org/10.1016/j.jwb.2013.11.011

[118] Mohr, T. (2014). *Playing Big*. New York, NY: Gotham Books.

[119] Quote from President Jimmy Carter from https://www.brainyquote.com/quotes/jimmy_carter_166073

[120] Turkay, S. (2014). *Setting Goals: Who, Why, How?* Manuscript. Harvard University. Retrieved from https://vpal.harvard.edu/publications/setting-goals-who-why-how

[121] Adams, Douglas. Quote from The Salmon of Doubt. Retrieved from https://www.goodreads.com/quotes/1398-i-love-deadlines-i-love-the-whooshing-noise-they-make

[122] GiveDirectly. Retrieved from https://givedirectly.org/

Chapter 11

[123] Burns, G. Quote retrieved from https://www.goodreads.com/quotes/275386-no-snowflake-in-an-avalanche-ever-feels-responsible

[124] Mager, R. (1988). *Making Instruction Work*. Belmont, CA: Lake Books.

Mager, R. (1999). *What Every Manager Should Know about Training* (2nd ed.). Atlanta, GA: The Center for Effective Performance.

[125] Mager, R. (1988). *Making Instruction Work*. Belmont, CA: Lake Books.

Mager, R. (1999). *What Every Manager Should Know about Training* (2nd ed.). Atlanta, GA: The Center for Effective Performance.

Chapter 12

[126] Shelton, J. Lyrics from *Love, Break Our Hearts.*

[127] Ashford, S. J., Blatt, R., & VandeWalle, D. (2003). Reflections on the looking glass: A review of research on feedback-seeking behavior organizations. *Journal of Management, 29*(6), 773–799.

https://doi.org/10.1016/S0149-2063(03)00079-5

[128] Nauert, R. (2012). Redefining Life Goals Can Foster Better Health. Retrieved June 9, 2018, from https://psychcentral.com/news/2012/04/24/redefining-life-goals-can-foster-better-health/37740.html

[129] Davis, M., Eshelman, E.R., & McKay, M. (1988). *The Relaxation and Stress Reduction Handbook*. Oakland, CA: New Harbinger Publications, Inc. The authors provide a comprehensive workbook on relaxation and stress reduction. My favorite part is the chart which highlights which techniques work for which symptoms of stress.

[130] Wood, A. M., Froh, J. J., & Geraghty, A. W. A. (2010). Clinical Psychology Review Gratitude and well-being: A review and theoretical integration. *Clinical Psychology Review, 30*(7), 890–905. https://doi.org/10.1016/j.cpr.2010.03.005

[131] O' Leary, K., & Dockray, S. (2015). The Effects of Two Novel Gratitude and Mindfulness Interventions on Well-Being. *The Journal of Alternative and Complementary Medicine, 21*(4), 243–245. https://doi.org/10.1089/acm.2014.0119

[132] Positive Psychology Program. (2017). What is Gratitude and What Is Its Role in Positive Psychology? Retrieved from https://positivepsychologyprogram.com/gratitude-appreciation/#effects

[133] Marcus, Erik. *Self-Care for Activists: A Guide to Clearing Yourself of Trauma While Working for a Better World* (Kindle Locations 430-432). Mocana Productions, Inc. Kindle Edition.

[134] Segran, Elizabeth. (2018). How A Beauty Brand Raised an Army Of 30,000 Political Activists. Fast Company. Retrieved from https://www.fastcompany.com/40540039/how-a-beauty-brand-raised-an-army-of-30000-political-activists

Made in the USA
Columbia, SC
14 April 2019